CAMBRIDGE

BALLS

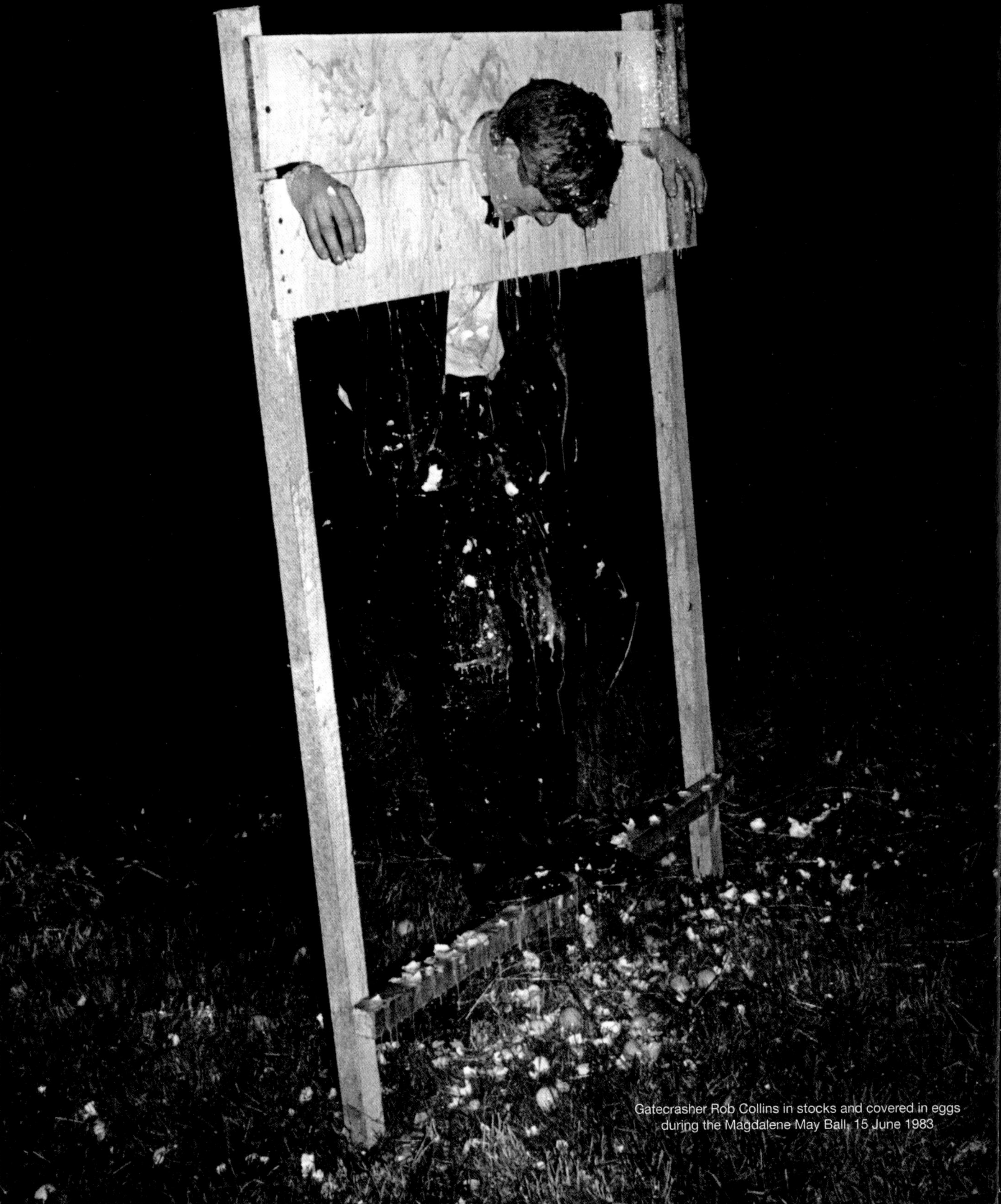

Gatecrasher Rob Collins in stocks and covered in eggs during the Magdalene May Ball, 15 June 1983

CAMBRIDGE

BALLS

PHOTOGRAPHS BY DAFYDD JONES

ACC ART BOOKS

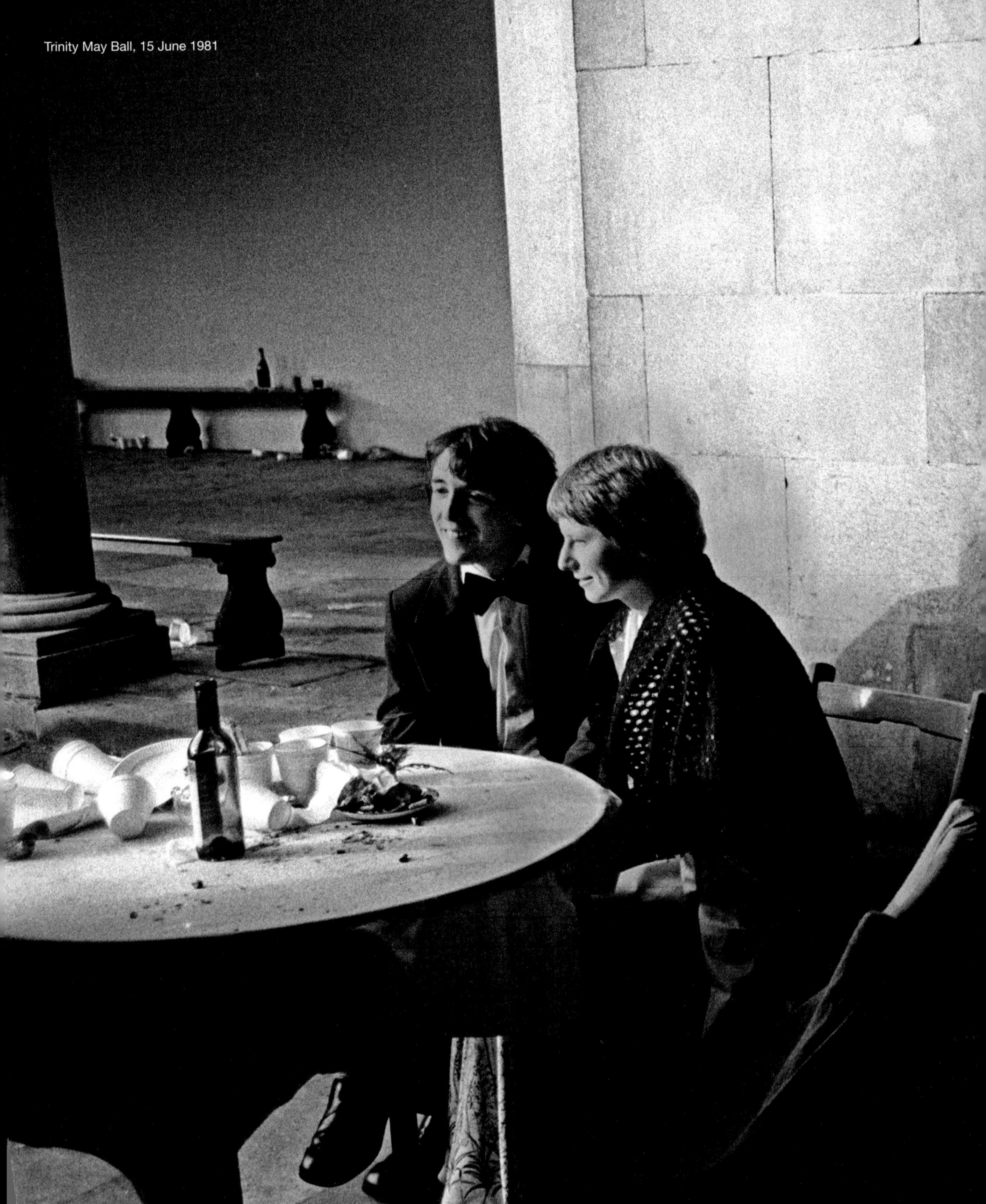
Trinity May Ball, 15 June 1981

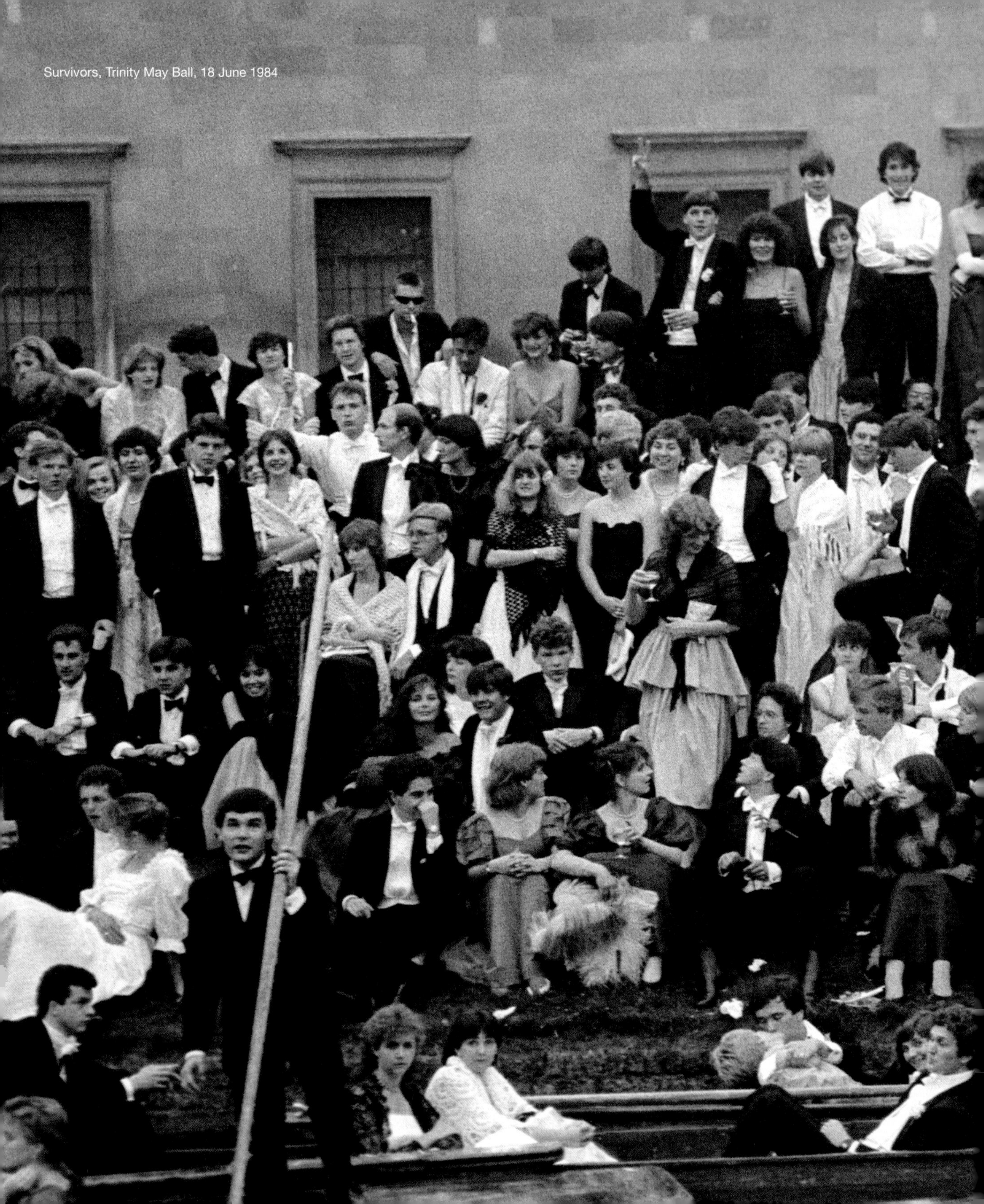

Survivors, Trinity May Ball, 18 June 1984

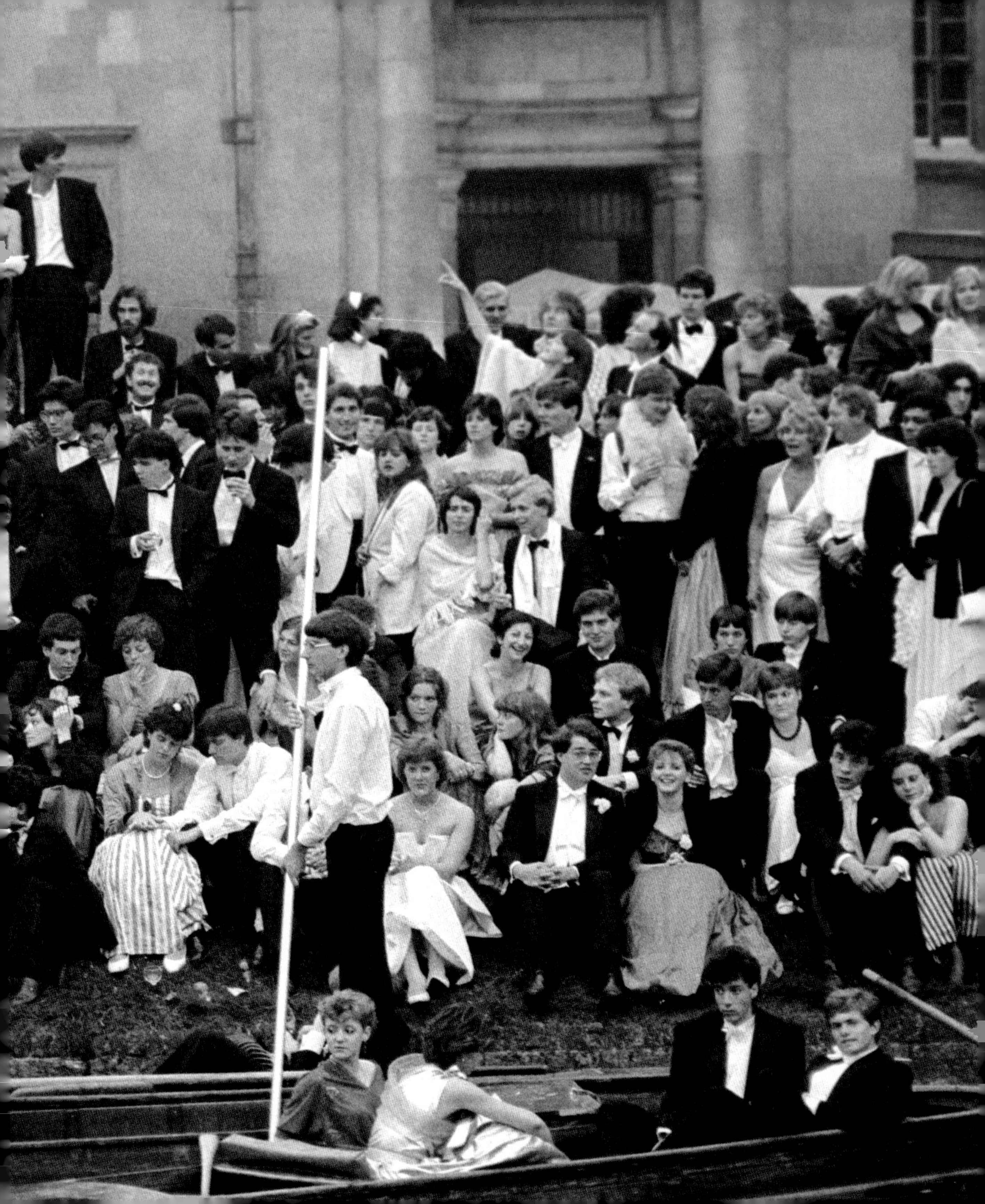

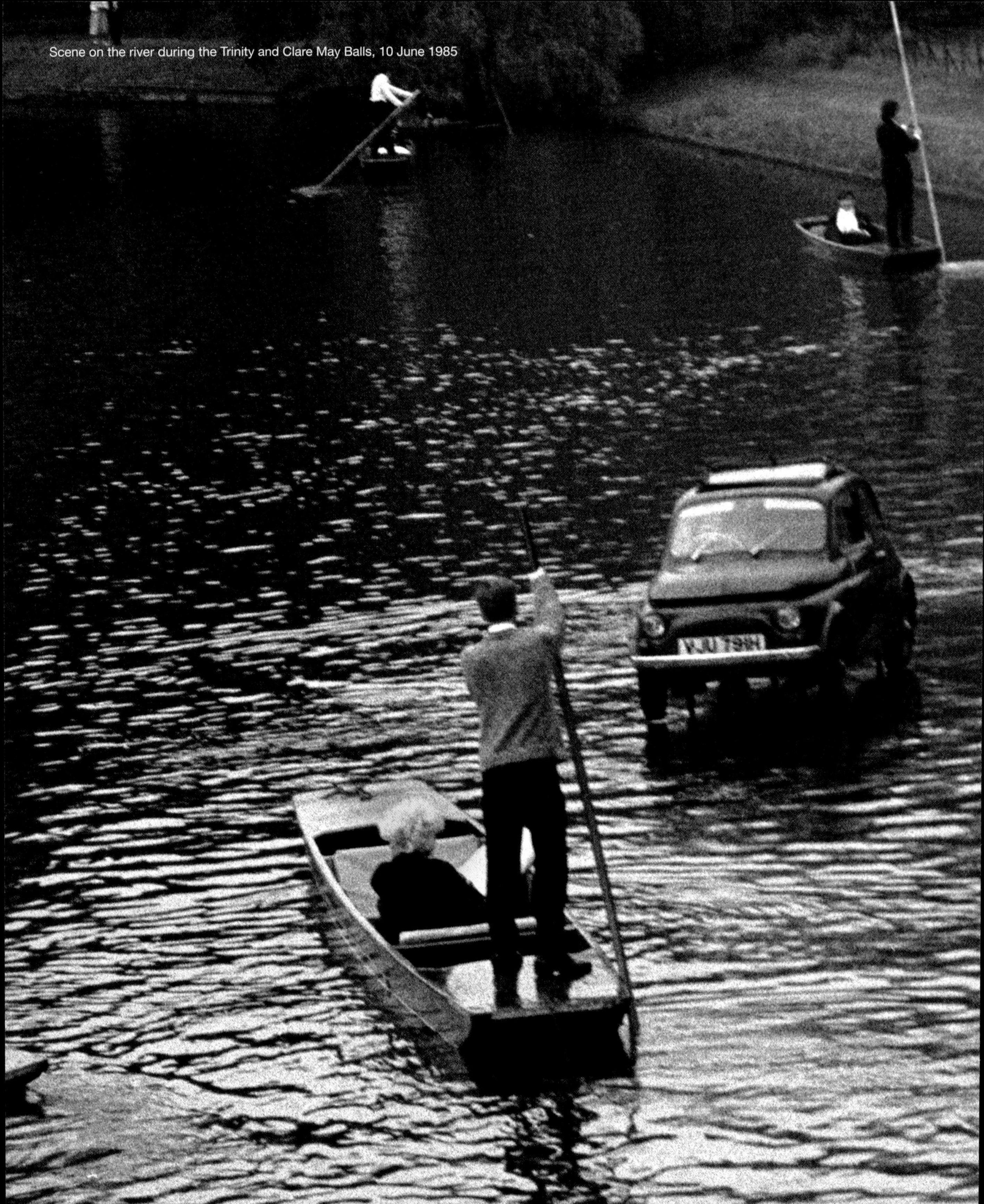

Scene on the river during the Trinity and Clare May Balls, 10 June 1985

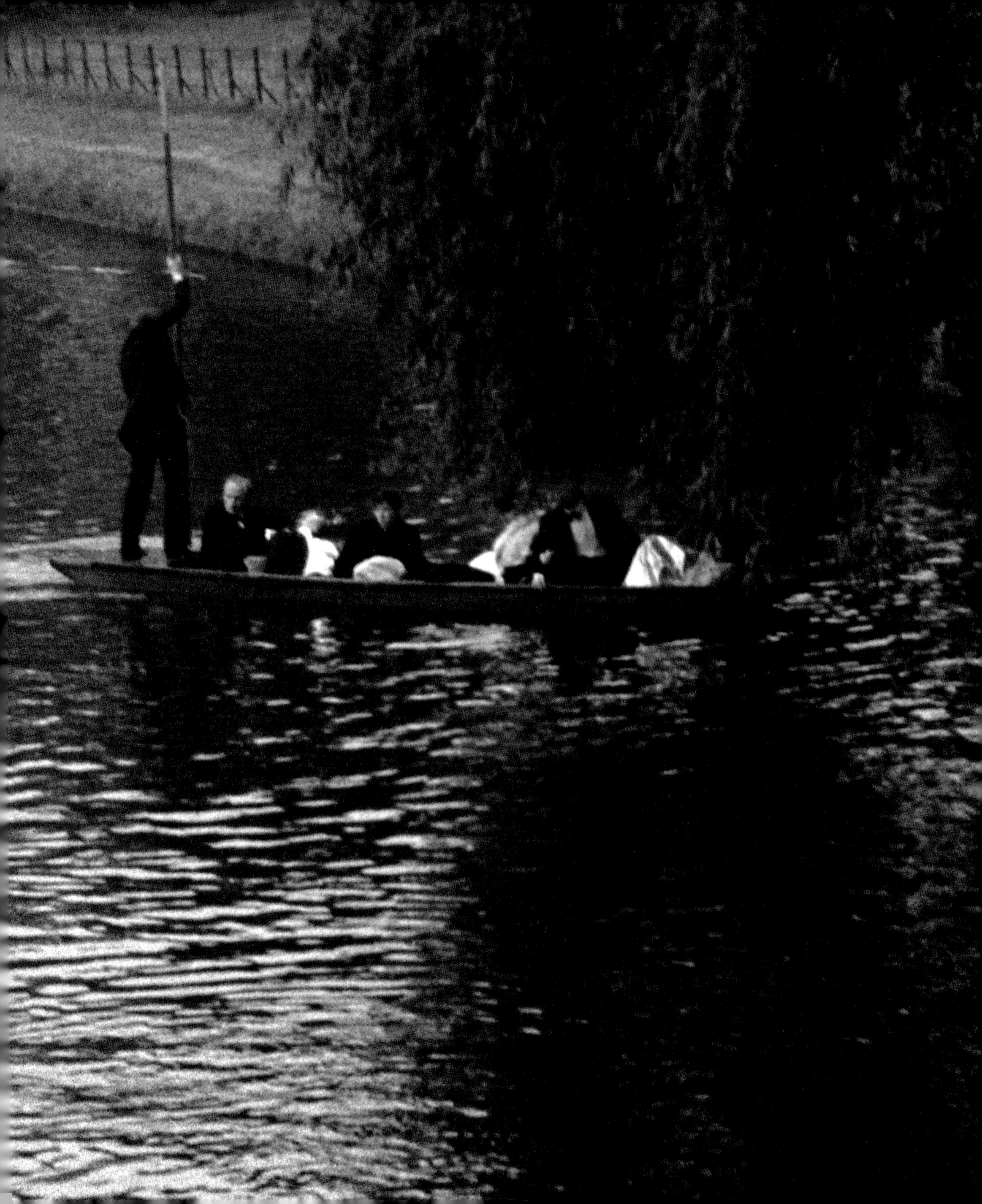

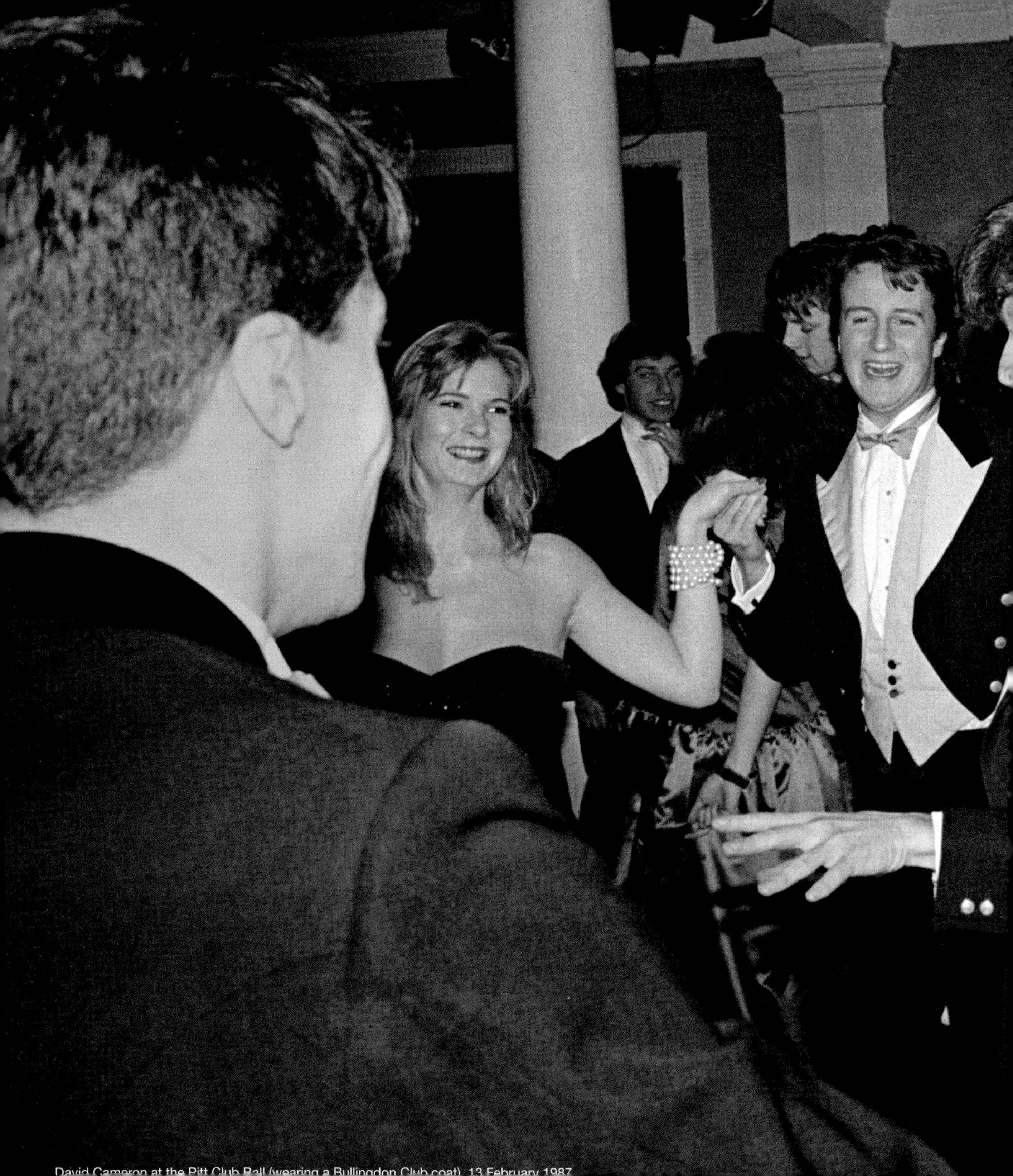

David Cameron at the Pitt Club Ball (wearing a Bullingdon Club coat), 13 February 1987

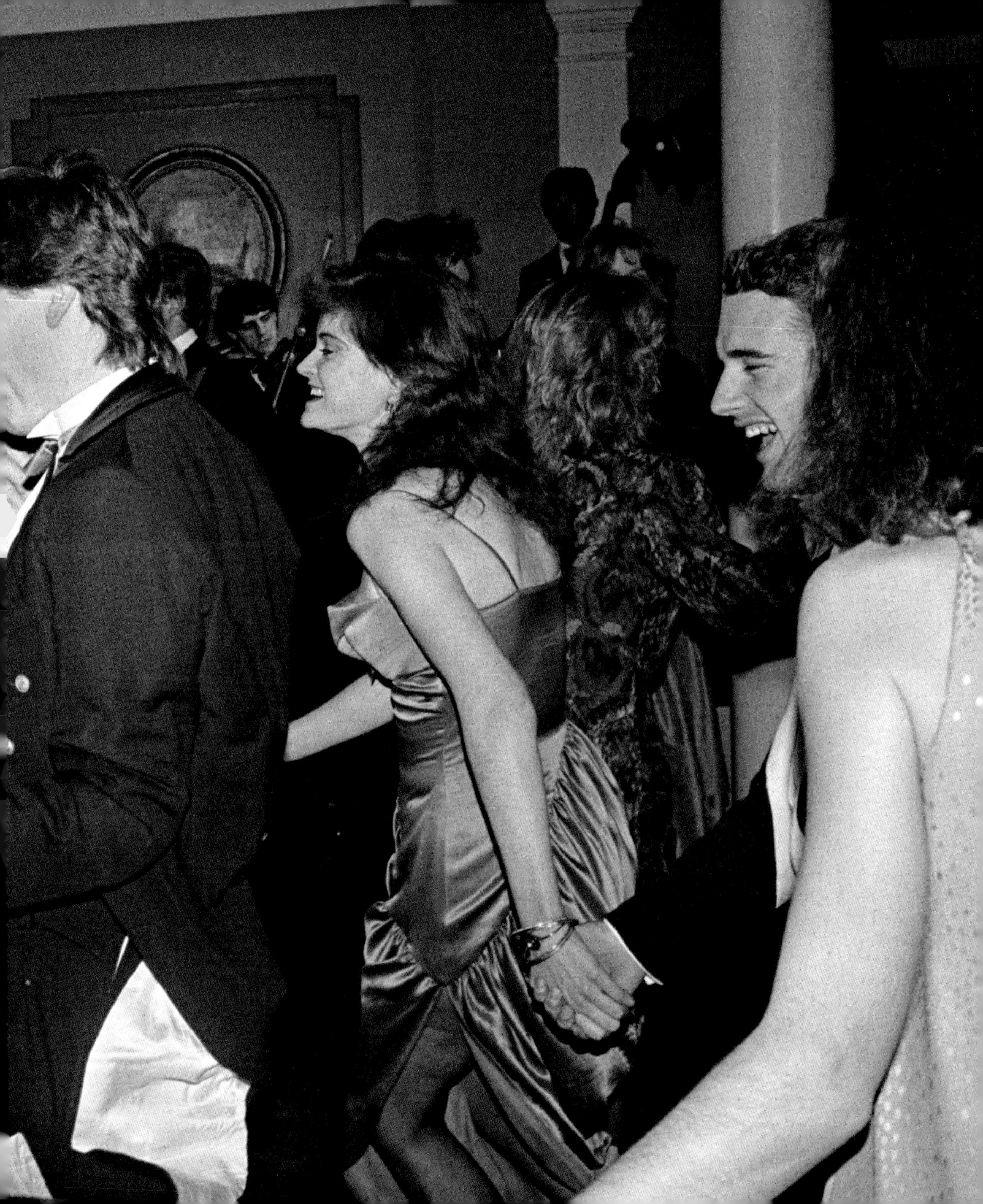

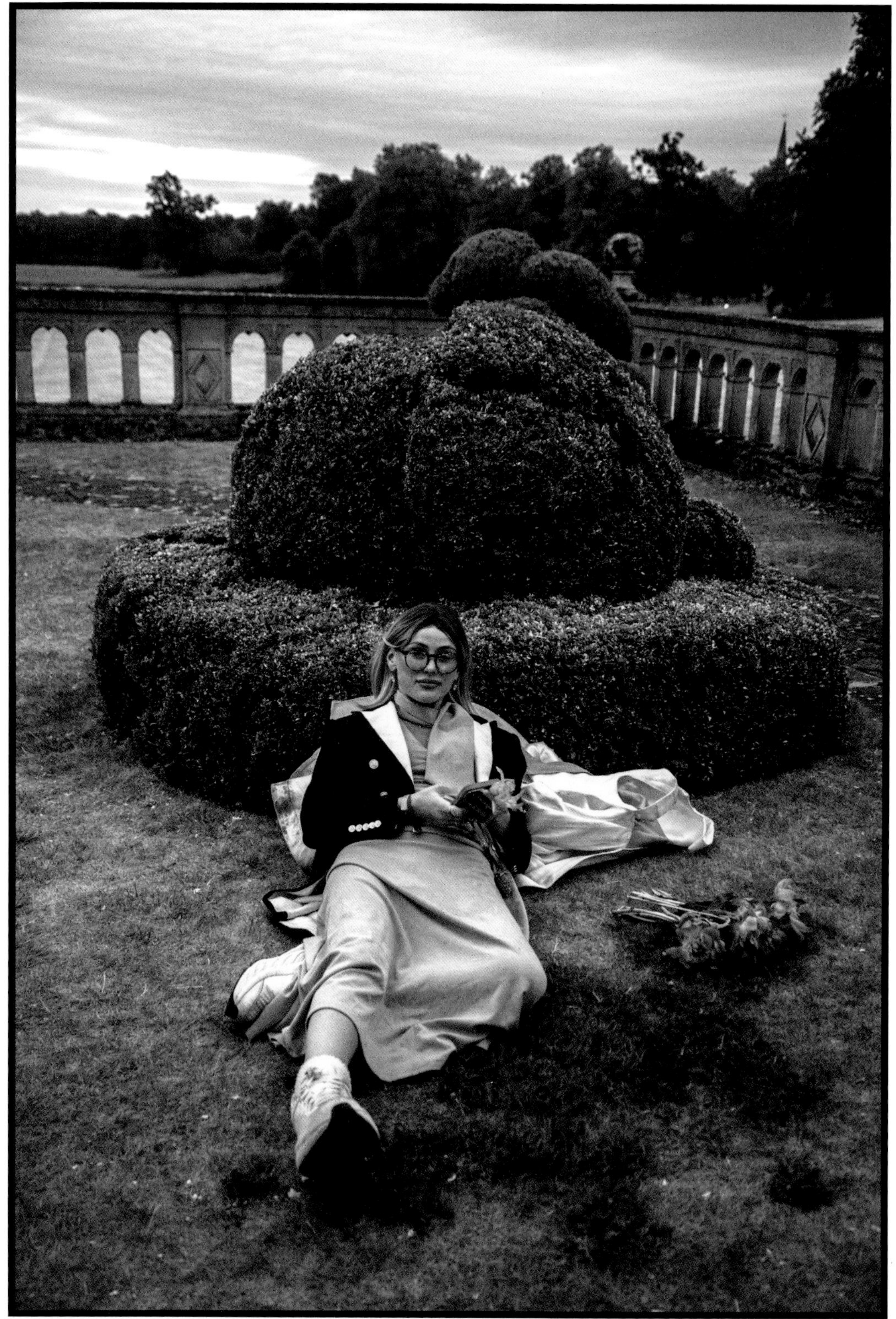

Caroline Calloway, Madingley Hall, 4.35 a.m., 24 June 2025

Foreword

If I could tell you one thing: Don't be jealous. Don't let this book make you feel like your life is boring. Like all the best parties are happening without you.

First of all, Dafydd and I aren't always invited to the parties we make art about, but more on that fascinating dynamic later! What I want you to know up front and above all else, is that, yes, truly—*just like you*—I was once sick to my fucking guts with envy when I thumbed through the exquisite Oxford ball photography of British living legend Dafydd Jones. Are all the better parties always in a different place? A different time? Should I have been born thirty years earlier? Seventy? A century? Two?!

That I am now writing the introduction for his Cambridge book is the honor of a lifetime—even makes me feel a flicker of deep gratitude I was born into exactly this one. You see, it'd be impossible to over-exaggerate how large Dafydd looms in the Oxbridge psyche. Most students know his work by name, but all of us have seen the famous photographs. David Cameron and Boris Johnson in their Buller tails, boats burning, a palanquin-ed Nigella Lawson, fireworks fanning out like weeping willows, party crashers punished like peasants in black tie, couples embraced in sleep and dew at dawn.

And of course, my favorite—the image I asked for in return for writing this: Hugh Grant at the absolute peak of his sly and stuttering sex appeal, dressed like a young satyr with grapes and leopard skins and twisted wicker horns, whispering into the neck of a girl with orchids in her hair. But still! I had questions about the man who could take such photographs! Was he a party animal himself? How did he always seem to ingratiate himself into the white-hot molten core of whatever party was going on around him? How did he always get such good shots?

They say never meet your heroes, but suddenly mine's wife was making me lunch. We were in East Sussex, at Dafydd's compound by the sea where his dark rooms and archives are housed in a nearby cottage on the property, a few days before our week of balls in Cambridge was about to begin. I had invited a handful of friends of all genders, sexual orientations, races, ages, and socio-economic backgrounds. And I wish I could say all white-haired British men of Dafydd's age are up to greet a social situation like this with the same open-hearted warmth and generosity of spirit that he did. But they're not. They're just not. In fact I've seen it all go horribly wrong before—had it go all horribly wrong all over me as some old man with a plummy accent and a signet ring condescended to me, or dismissed me, or—*the worst*—openly pitied or mocked me when I told him that I write about girlhood and I take photos of girlhood and I do all of this on my iPhone because I have enough Instagram followers to make this work. A lot of white-haired British men of Dafydd's age have very old-fashioned ideas about what the quality of such creative output must be like (slop) and very sexist ideas about what kind of woman would choose this life. Think: attention-whore, narcissist. Never: Artist.

But not Dafydd! He listened to my stories about Instagram and Cambridge in the mid 2010's with the same rapt attention our group gave him when he told us his significantly more interesting anecdotes about working for *Tatler*'s Tina Brown and *Vanity Fair*'s Graydon Carter in the late 80's. From the moment he met my friends Dafydd was kind, gracious, ushering us through his renovated farmhouse with a bubbling tray of coupes and flutes, pointing out his vegetable beds and his binders full of favorite photographs, all the while smiling sheepishly under our very American barrage of compliments. He was quieter than I expected. Almost shy. And I realized all at once that I'd been doing it wrong this entire time: I got into the rooms I wanted to photograph by becoming a main character. Dafydd, I suspected, knew how to disappear.

And I was right. After lunch that day at his house, we set out with my friends on what can only be described as "a poorly panned week of balls." Who planned them? Well, I did, of course! Someone had to and I actually would have preferred that someone else *had*, but no one else believed we could fit so many parties into so little time. And so, I took our overbooked schedule into my very incompetent and optimistic hands. Only here's the thing: Not all balls wanted to invite us! It's true. Gone were the days when my friends were organizing all the parties. I had now entered an early era of my career that Dafydd assured me he, too, had encountered at my age and still did—at times—bump up against to this day. Here was the problem: Because both he and I were famous for taking party pictures, not all ball committees saw our presence as an asset. To a select few, we were liabilities. Mostly we were honored guests, seated head of the table, jumping queues, there with our cameras to add to the overall cultural ambience and historical significance of the night, but I've never been afraid to say exactly what I mean when it comes to Cambridge. Trinity this year, despite my emails, wouldn't let us in.

Dafydd assured me they had always been "funny" with him, but this rejection was new to me and I did not like it. I'd been part of the Cambridge Night Climbers and had broken into countless balls for sport, always knowing the option of buying a ticket was there to catch me like a spotter if I needed it, but this? Breaking in because I *had* to? Thirty-three felt too old for wigs, but I put the disguise on anyways because I am just the amount of famous that people recognize me with orchids in my hair, but with bangs and glasses no one has ever seen my face before in their entire goddamn lives.

One of my favorite photographs of me is the one Dafydd took right after I broke in. I had left my friends to enjoy the final forty minutes of the ball and cabbed it back to meet him by the fountain in the gardens at Madingley Hall. In the photo, I'm lying in the wet grass, doom-scrolling, flowers I'd stolen from the Trinity decorations scattered around me like the most glamorous trash, trying so hard to look like someone else and yet Dafydd captured me precisely. Our plan that morning was this: Dafydd would drive us the five minutes back into town in his car and then he would photograph all the white-tied students stumbling drunkenly home. Me? I would "shadow" him. What did that mean? Um. I wasn't sure, exactly. But it sounded official and Dafydd had agreed and I was certain that I wanted to.

And my God. What a shitty, shitty dawn! I've seen sweeping, searing sunrises stream over these spires, but this was one of those humid, gloomy, drizzling days where the sky just goes all milky and sad and pale. The only worse luck for weather would be a thunderstorm. I had purposefully paced myself with drinks at Trinity so I wouldn't be too wasted for this, but as we stepped out of his car into mud and light drizzles with no umbrellas or boots, I started to regret my own sobriety. I was cold, tired. I wanted more alcohol. I wanted Dafydd to slow down. Dafydd was *fast*. I'm a bitch who always wears sneakers under my ball gown so I'm ready for anything, but this little British tuxedoed man was *moving*. Over bridges, down alleyways, through gardens and short-cuts and canopied paths. He didn't know this city, but he would ask me where certain landmarks or colleges were, and I would point, and then he would be off again. I was somehow both directing us *and* following him, becoming suddenly more alert but not more content as I watched his body language change.

Dafydd was in a flow state now. And I...? I was okay, I guess. Fine, really. Because here's the thing: Everything sucked, okay? The ball had been mid. Not being invited

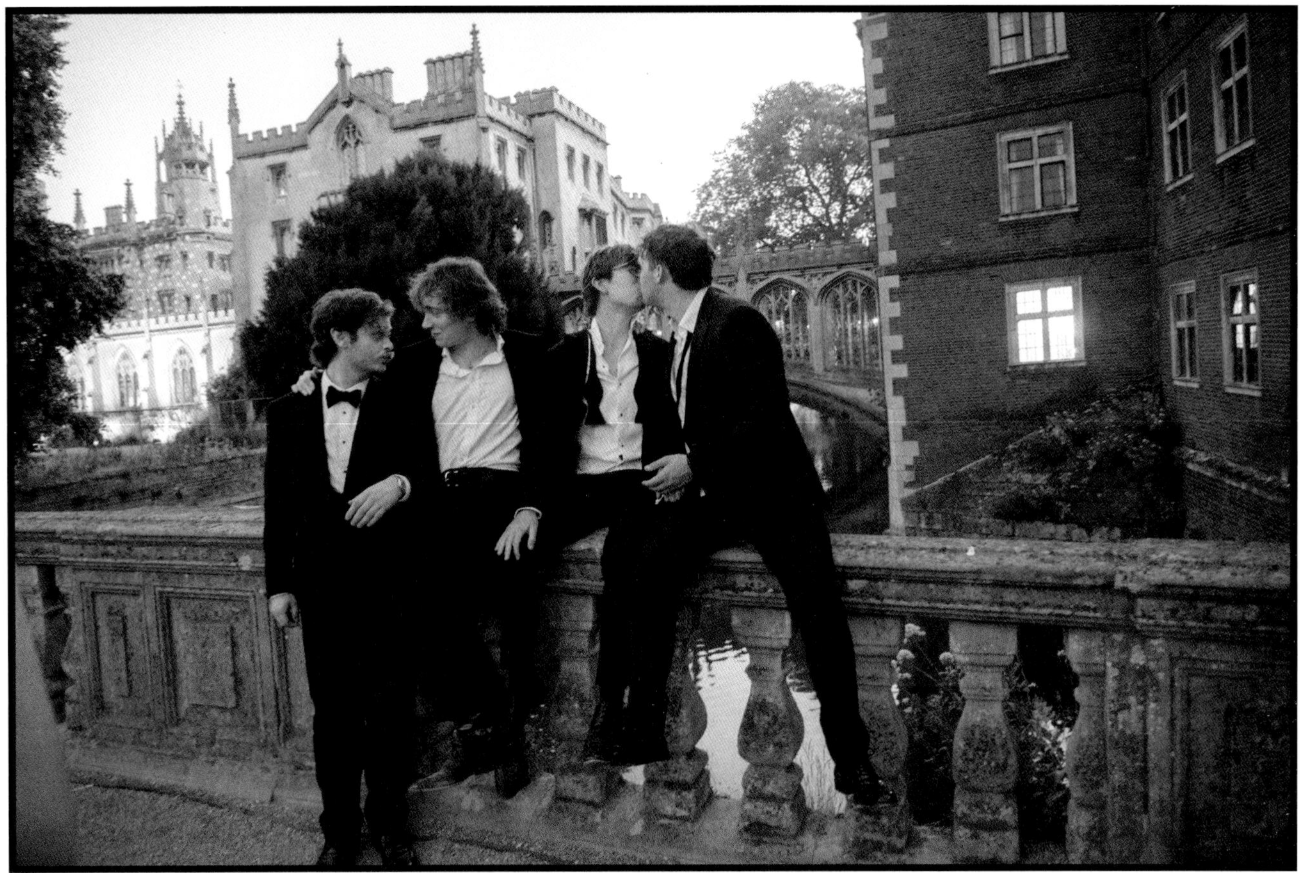

for the first time had seriously hurt my feelings. Breaking in had been a stressful last resort. My friends are getting older. And here I was, sleepy and too sober and damp. Nothing around me seemed magical, but I could tell by Dafydd's expression and posture and pace that he was loving all the stuff he was shooting so, so much. Boys with their bow ties undone and their arms around each other, singing. A couple making out on a cobblestone curb, his jacket around her shoulders. A ball gown poofing and then sinking as the girl's bare feet and legs hit the water of the River Cam.

But that's the secret: It's the photographer who makes the magic, not the magical moment that makes a great photograph. Dafydd has two super powers he employs to summon this immense beauty out of the ether. Sometimes he blends in to the point of invisibility so he can get close to the action. But sometimes he takes the wettest, dreariest, most boring dawn and magicks it into *art*. So please. Don't be jealous. Don't let this book make you feel like your life is boring. Like all the best parties are happening without you. Even the people at these parties wish they were living in another age sometimes. Dark academia TikTok yearns for 2016 millennial cringe or perhaps Dafydd's older photographs. The people in Dafydd's photographs and perhaps dark academia TikTok are all imitating the *Brideshead Revisited* miniseries. The book by Evelyn Waugh mourns the lost luxury of parties before World War I, and so on.

Caroline Calloway
Sarasota, Florida
October 2025

St John's May Ball, 24 June 2025

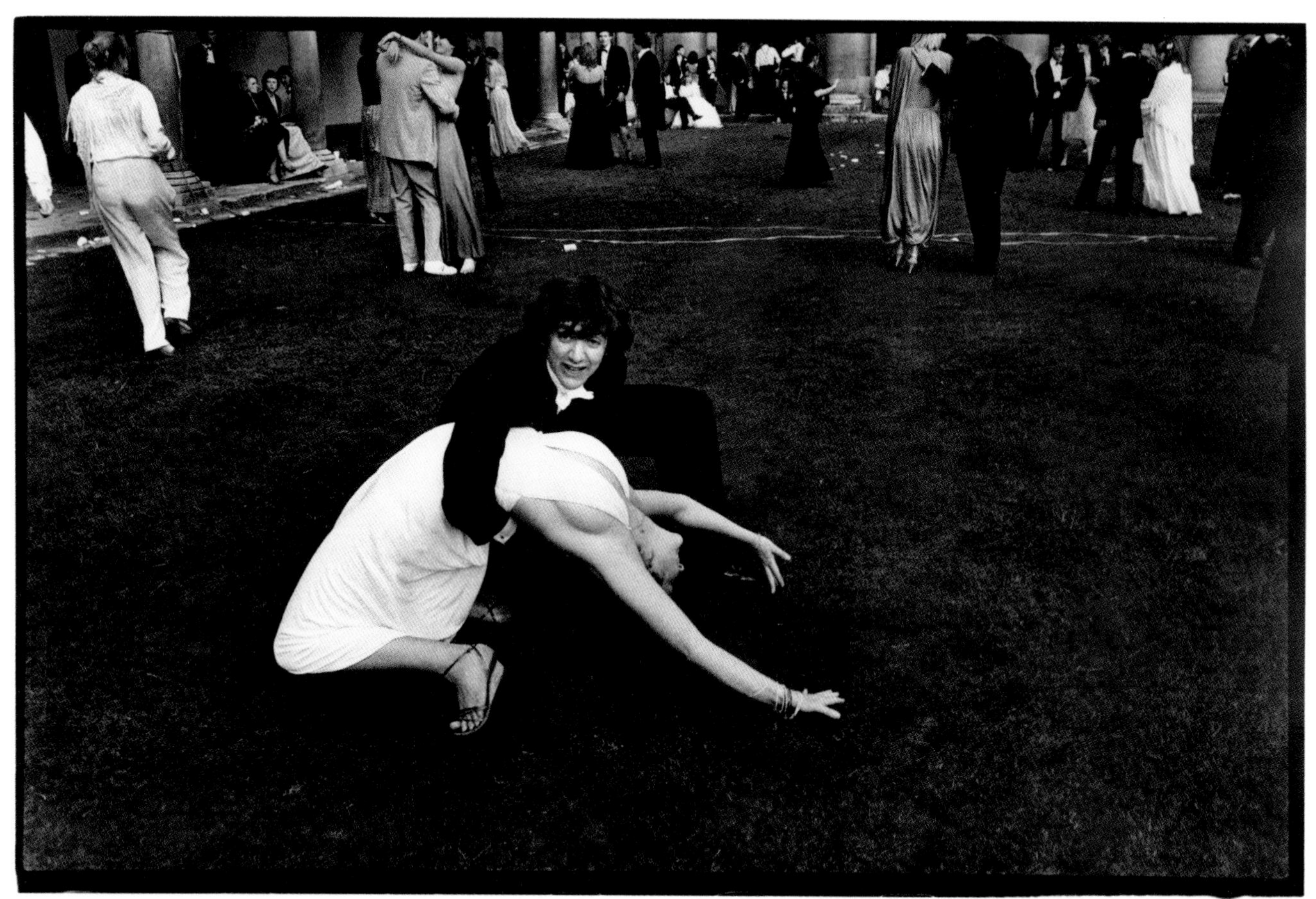

Alexander Fyjis-Walker dancing with Sarah Fazakerly during the Trinity May Ball, 15 June 1981

Introduction

In 1981 England was in a recession. There were riots. Factories were closing. Unemployment was high. I had set up as a photographer in a shared studio in Oxford. I had little work but my pictures of dining clubs and students dressing up at parties had been recently published in the *Sunday Times* magazine under the headline 'The Return of the Bright Young Things'.

I'd travelled to Cambridge early in my search for Bright Young Things but found none at the Pitt Club Ball. It was more old-fashioned and less sophisticated than its Oxford equivalent: the culmination of the event was the blowing of hunting horns. The Cambridge colleges seemed to have much less social activity going on during the year. But I was told they really went to town for their renowned end-of-year 'May' balls – perversely always held in June.

I scraped together the money for the train fare and turned up in Cambridge with no lodgings for the night, the clothes I stood up in, a small Olympus camera and several rolls of bulk loaded black-and-white film. I thought it was an interesting hidden world to photograph. No one was paying me to go. I just thought the pictures might be good.

On the whole, students studying don't make for exciting pictures. Yet at their final balls, not only were the party-goers celebrating the end of their exams but the balls were milestones in their lives, which would never be the same again.

I arrived in time for the Trinity May Ball at the beginning of the week. Trinity traditionally has a major ball that starts off the week's celebrations. Of course, I had no ticket so, at first, I explored outside the college walls photographing the gatecrashers, some of whom were climbing in while others were crossing the river in punts. By the time the sun was rising I could just walk in. Although some had fallen asleep, the exotically named Sarah Fazakerley and Alexander Fyjis-Walker were dancing exuberantly.

There, I met a photographer friend Nicholas Lee who offered me a place to sleep the day afterwards, at his place in Histon.

On Wednesday it was the Magdalene College ball. They had a reputation for having the most glamorous, traditional ball with champagne flowing all night. It was one of the most expensive and exclusive tickets – £60 for a double ticket. Only 500 ball-goers.

The ball tickets were open to students at the college, fellows and alumnae. Each could invite a guest. I'd managed to organise access. My name was on a slip of paper at the Porters' Lodge.

By this time, I'd realised there was no point staying up all night since the pictures I wanted would be taken after dawn in the early morning light. I slept well then turned up at 4.30 a.m. on the Thursday morning. The ball-goers had been dancing and partying all night. By now there was a calmness amongst the languorous, beautiful ball-goers lounging on the lawn in the Master's Garden and by the river. *Tatler* magazine was already covering this ball and had commissioned their own photographer – the latter had been photographing all night and was therefore flagging by the early hours. When Tina Brown, the editor, heard that I had been there too she called, wanting to see my pictures. The result was a spread in *Tatler* that ran with the headline 'Cambridge Holds Its Balls and Dances', the publication of which helped lead to a prized actual job as a *Tatler* photographer.

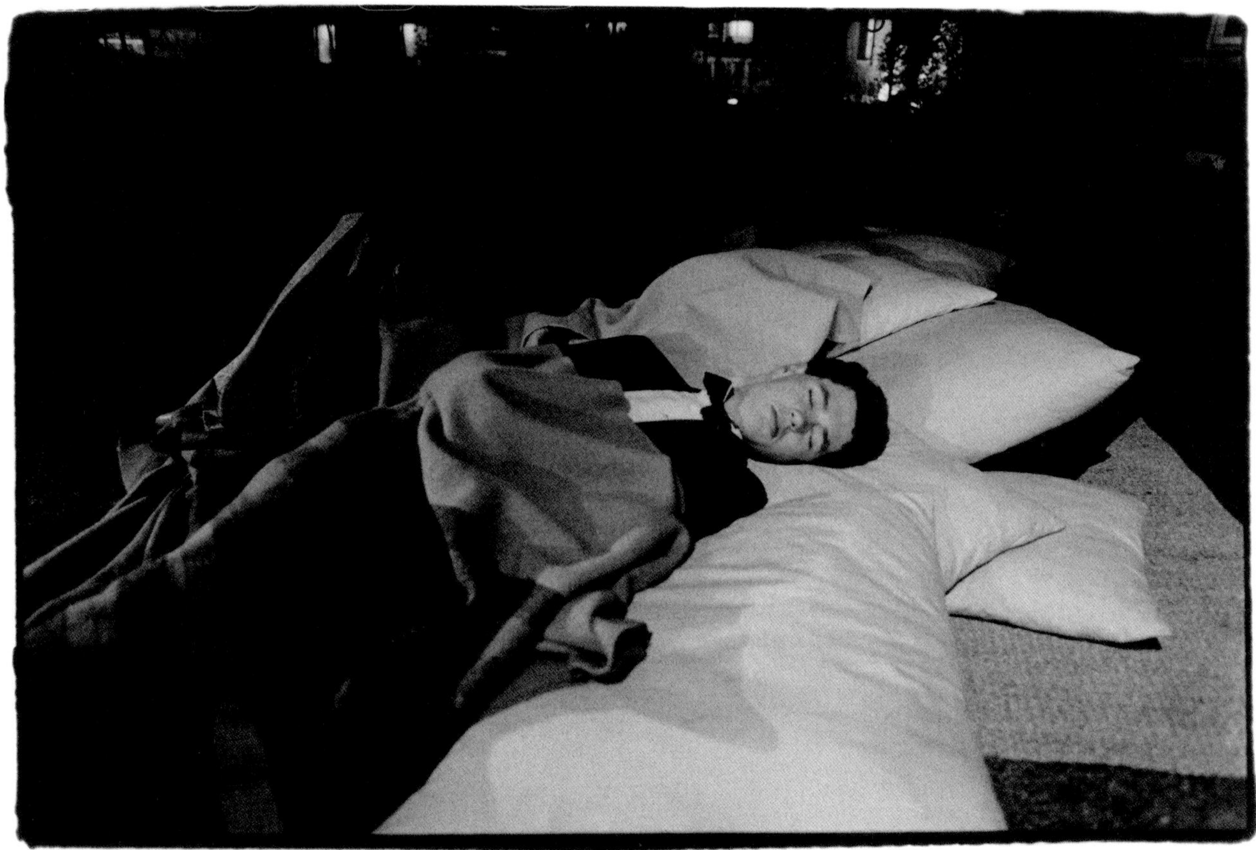

This new professional role gave me a continuing entrée to events in Cambridge. The magazine office organised the invitations for me. I was invited back to balls and drinks parties there every year.

I observed the charisma and enthusiasm of various emerging young talents among the student body, such as historian (now Lord) Andrew Roberts, writer Simon Sebag Montefiore, Samantha Weinberg and Orlando Fraser who were all busy social figures. One year I was invited to the Wylie drinks. The drinking club had been banned from the vicinity of Cambridge University, so they had their drinks party on Grantchester Meadows. The idea was to get very drunk. I also photographed David Cameron wearing his Bullingdon coat at a Pitt Club Ball in Cambridge. From another age, The Pitt, a private members' club in a beautiful neo-classical building on Jesus Lane in the middle of Cambridge, had historically been the social centre for the poshest of the aristocratic students. It was still going strong in the 1980s but by the early 2000s The Pitt was considered uncool and embarrassing. It was so behind the times it was not until 2017 that women were allowed to join.

One year a cock-up at the *Tatler* office resulted in my covering the Trinity HALL Ball, not the Trinity College Ball. It was a smaller less glamorous occasion and when I arrived

Trinity Hall May Ball, 1983

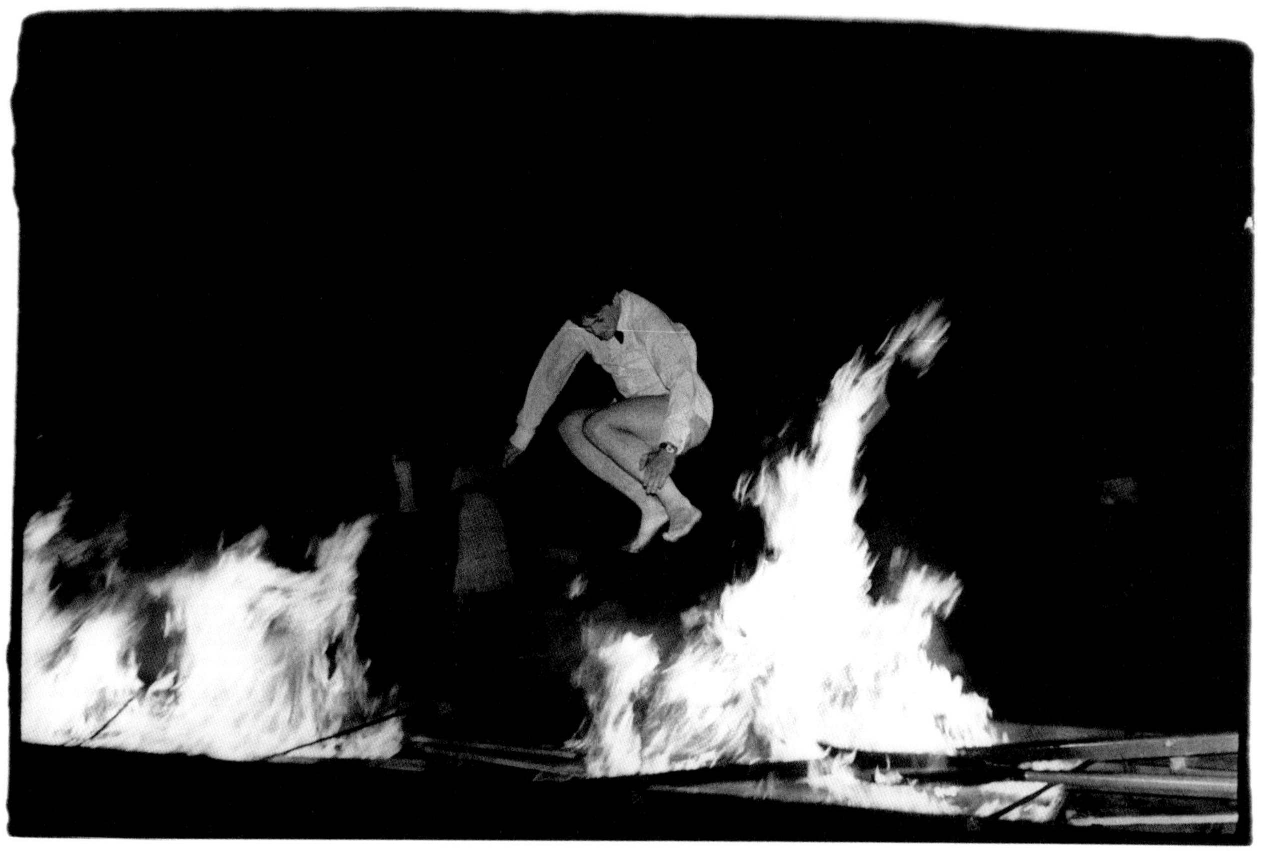

many of the guests seemed to be already asleep. However, I took some of my favourite sleeper pictures there.

Another year Magdalene College had set up some stocks and a large number of eggs in cartons nearby so that gatecrashers could be imprisoned in the stocks and the ball-goers had fun throwing eggs at them. After their ordeal – which they bore good-naturedly, they would be released and allowed to remain at the ball and enjoy it.

At Oxford and Cambridge, crews train for months for the annual rowing competitions between colleges. Traditionally, the winning crew would have a celebratory dinner afterwards. After the dinner a boat would be set alight, and rowers would jump over the flames. It was a kind of tribal tradition. (There was a similar tradition at Oxford.) This not only appeared to be but actually was reckless and dangerous.

In fairness to the women, who had bare legs and therefore risked greater injury, the men took their trousers off before jumping.

One year most fire extinguishers were hidden in case of misuse. Just one was left out in case of an accident, with a predictable outcome.

Burning Boats, Downing College, 1984

One Saturday afternoon I took a break from the smoky parties and went for a healthy afternoon out with the Cambridge Beaglers whose tradition was to roll over hedges – rather than walk through gates – for which the right type of tweed jacket needed to be worn.

At some of the balls there would be a raucous atmosphere culminating around the darkest time of the night. People don't always have a good time at parties; sometimes they get into quite bad depressions. After midnight was the peak time for these moods. I wanted to photograph this too but also had to tread carefully. If anyone objected to being photographed, I would leave them alone.

In 1991 a publicist invited me to come to a concert by a new band the Manic Street Preachers who were due to play at the May Ball of Downing College. The band played just one very loud song and then began smashing up the PA equipment. The event turned out to be a PR stunt; the college was being played for publicity as it was intended to deliver pictures showing the band rebelling against the 'posh toff' students in dinner jackets.

I was an outsider but still thought Oxbridge was wonderful. The historic buildings, the libraries, the rivers, the traditions and clothing, the dreamy early morning mists, the brilliant minds and the academic enthusiasm.

There was a kind of fix. Parents could pay for a private education and thereby hugely increase the chances of their child finishing off their education at Oxbridge, which in the eighties and nineties was free.

Full disclosure: In 2008, our son, Lewis, went to King's College, Cambridge to study architecture.

We had always lived in very urban environments – Brooklyn and South London. His impression was that Cambridge was like a kind of theme park. The city full of tourists looking through railings at students in beautiful country-house-type colleges as though at animals in a zoo.

Punting is now a kind of local service industry. In the past, students would punt themselves, often with hilarious accidents. Now, there are professional punters. The local punt-hire firms employ strong young men from the city to do the punting, reminiscent of Venetian gondoliers. Which adds to the impression of Cambridge as some kind of luxury theme park.

As a dad, I would travel up to Cambridge. I could see that there were fewer of the old type of privileged aristocrats. That elite group had been outclassed by international students from 1 per cent backgrounds. Over the last 40 years the intake from Eton College seems to have roughly halved. Now, there are far more postgraduate, international and women students.

A German postgraduate student currently at Oxford University slightly regretfully told me the 'crazy English' public schoolboys of the 1980s are outnumbered. That social division which used to be between public and state school-educated students has now switched to a separation between the wealthy international students and often poorer English ones.

Today's generations of Oxbridge students have no need for someone from *Tatler* to document their lives. They are very used to photographing themselves. It is quite difficult to take journalistic-type pictures because everyone has a camera-ready face for pictures and already posts on social media. Caroline Calloway originally became a celebrity/influencer because of her fairy tale-like social media posts about being a student at Cambridge.

I was a guest in one of her punt rides with friends along the river – a journey much filmed and photographed. Then we all went to the King's College celebration. There, they go against the grain and hold a ball where the tickets are more reasonably priced and students can wear what they like and come in fancy dress.

One of the side effects of social media and smart phone addiction seems to be that the sexes are not as interested in each other as they used to be. Also, something else is happening that I can't help noticing in the rest of society. I call it the rise of single-sex groups. Groups of men or women partying together. In the eighties there would have been couples. Women were often guests invited to the ball but not studying at the university. Now, the previously all-male colleges have women studying too.

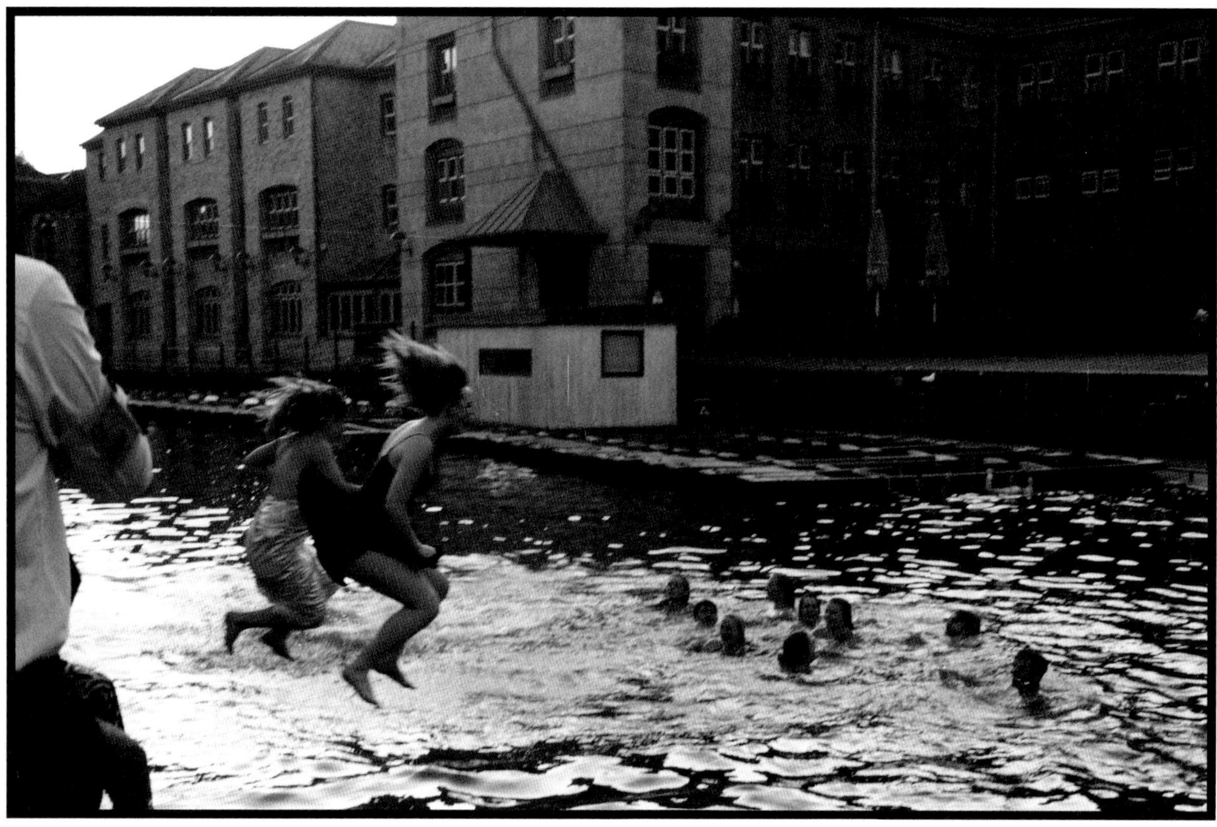

Magdalene College voted to admit women in 1988. The last all-male college to do so.

I returned to the Magdalene Ball twice in recent years. In 2023 we were having yet another heatwave and it was a very warm balmy morning-after. There was a difference at the end of the ball. Unlike previous decades when a couple of rugby player-type guys couldn't resist jumping off the nearby bridge over the river to celebrate at the end of the ball, this time a large number of women exuberantly led the way into the river fully clothed.

The celebration was more special because they were of the generation that had suffered from various lockdowns early in their studies. Imagine starting a university career in a new town and having to be confined to your room and not allowed to socialise. They had survived everything and were celebrating finishing the year. Some young men followed the women. They seemed more concerned about their expensive morning suits and carefully removed them first. The women just jumped in…

Magdalene May Ball, 21 June 2023

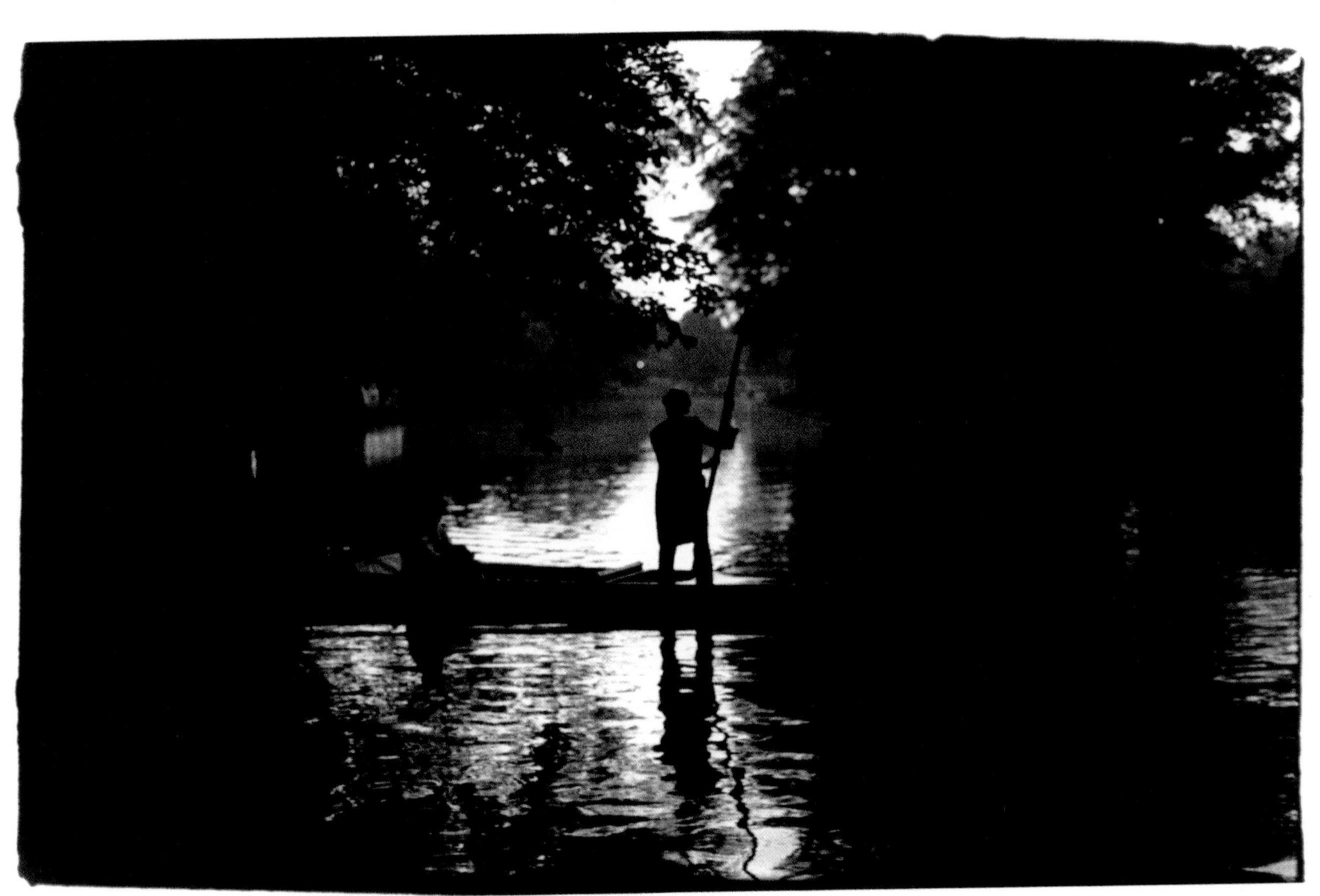

Magdalene May Ball, 15 June 1983

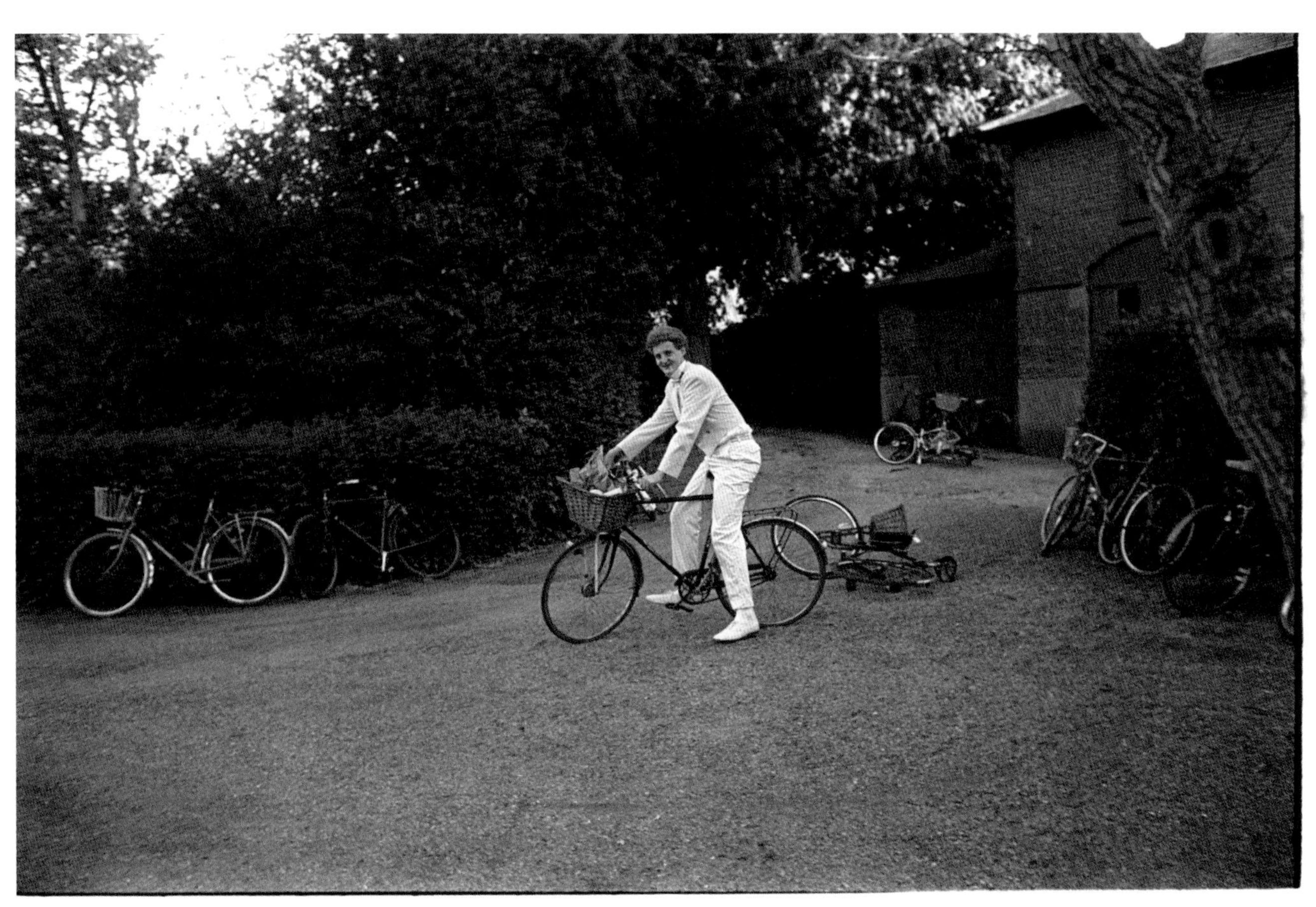

Adrian Leslie, Porterhouse Blue Party, May 1984

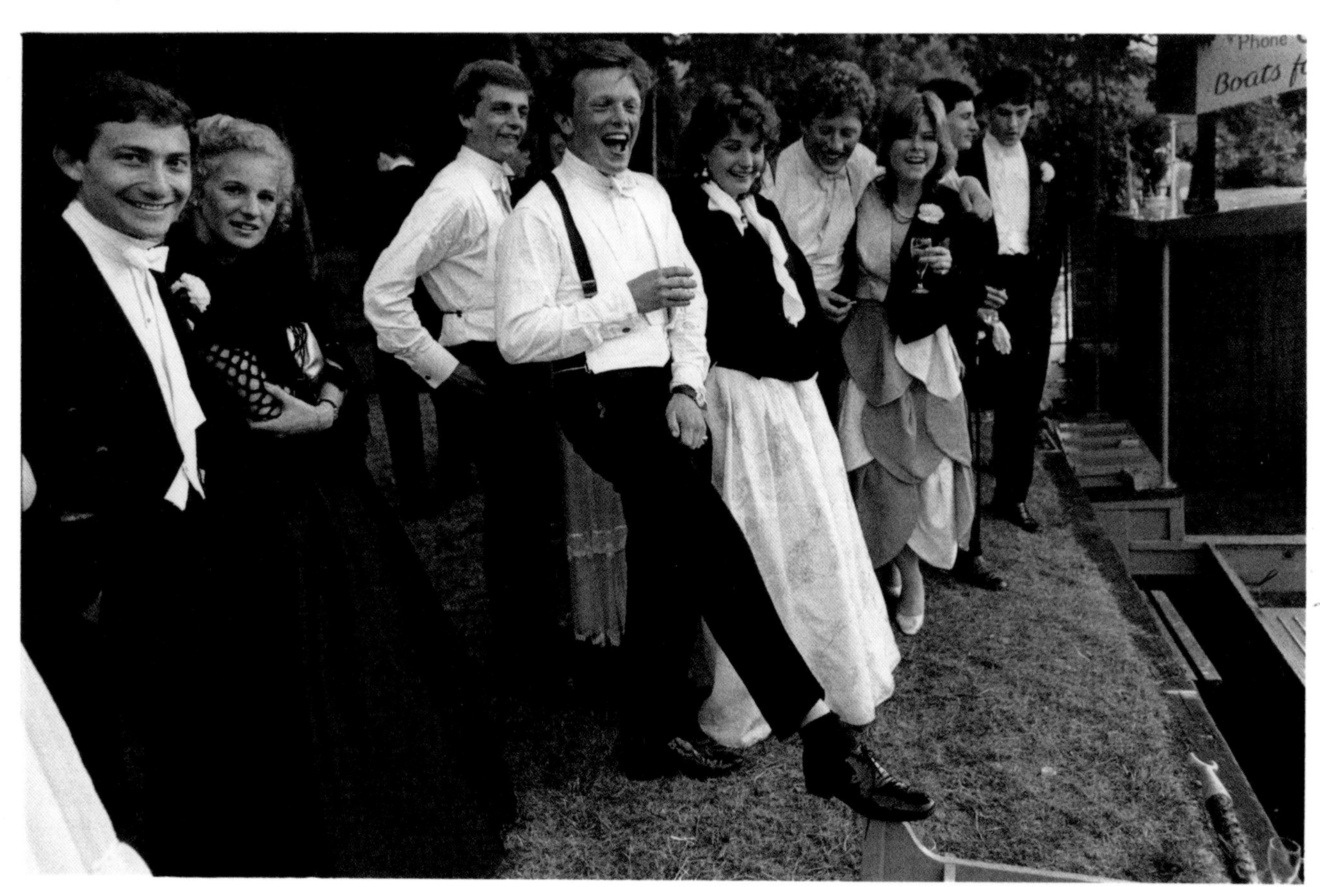

Magdalene May Ball, 15 June 1983

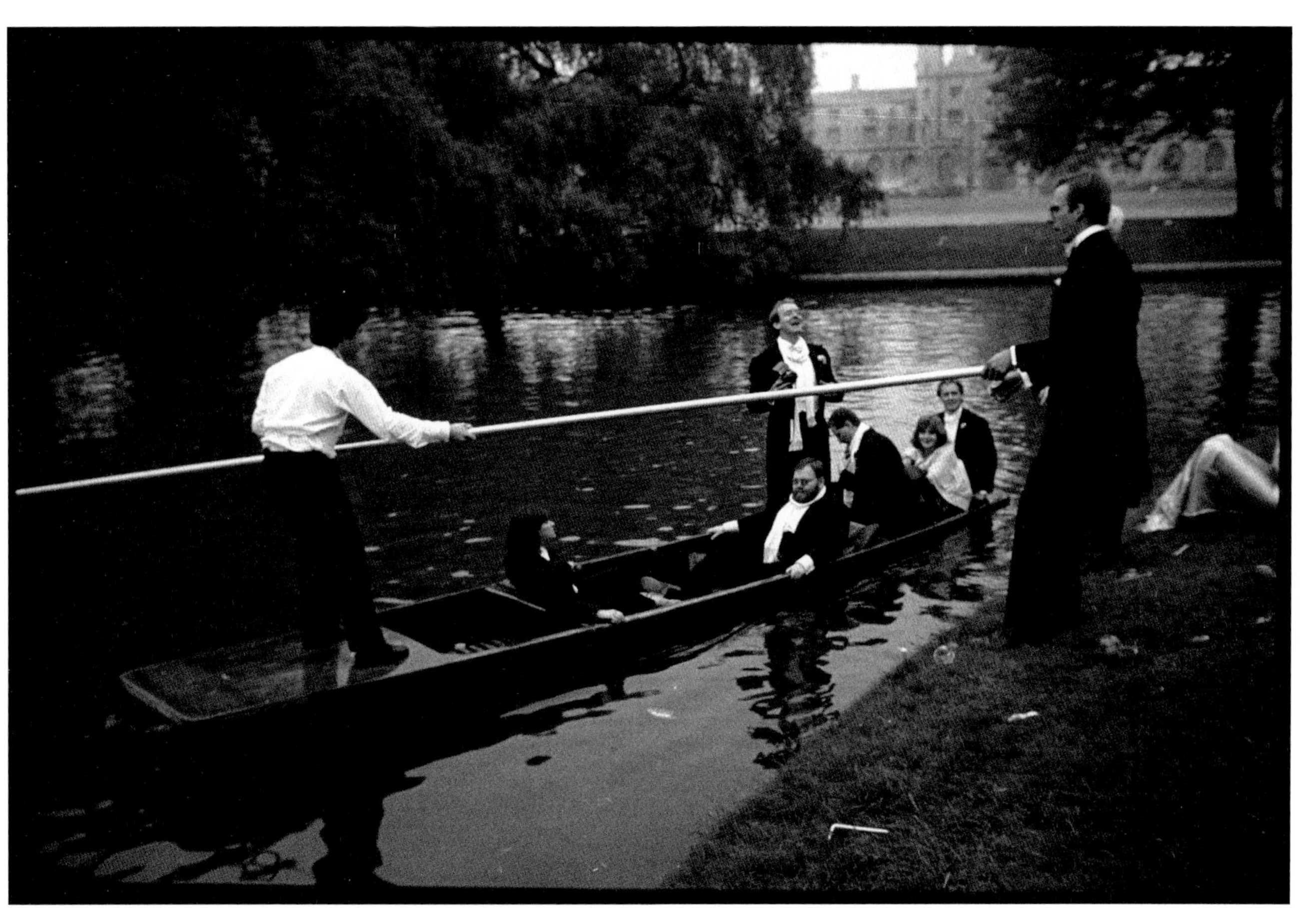

Punting after the Trinity May Ball, 18 June 1984

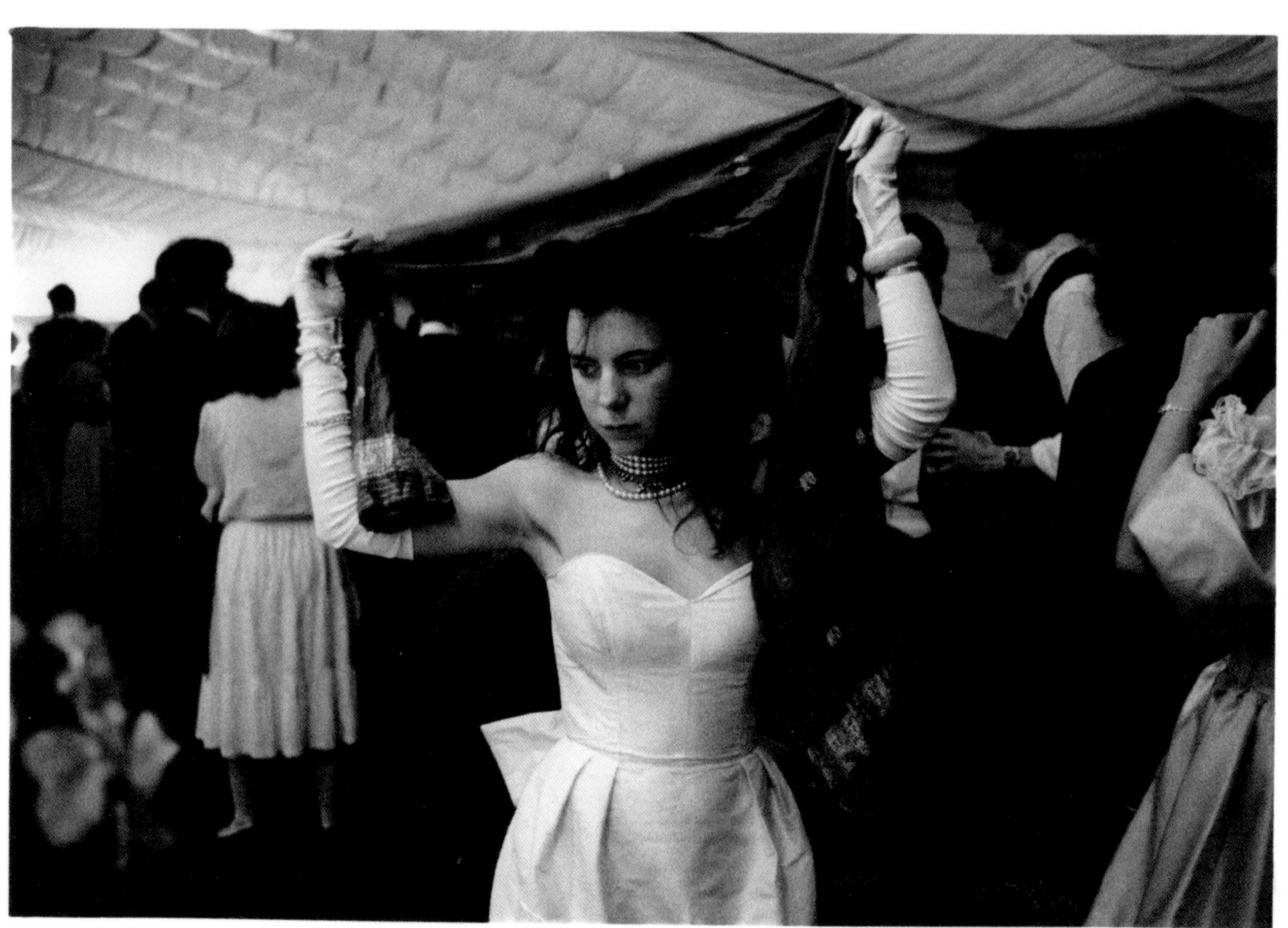

Magdalene May Ball, 15 June 1983

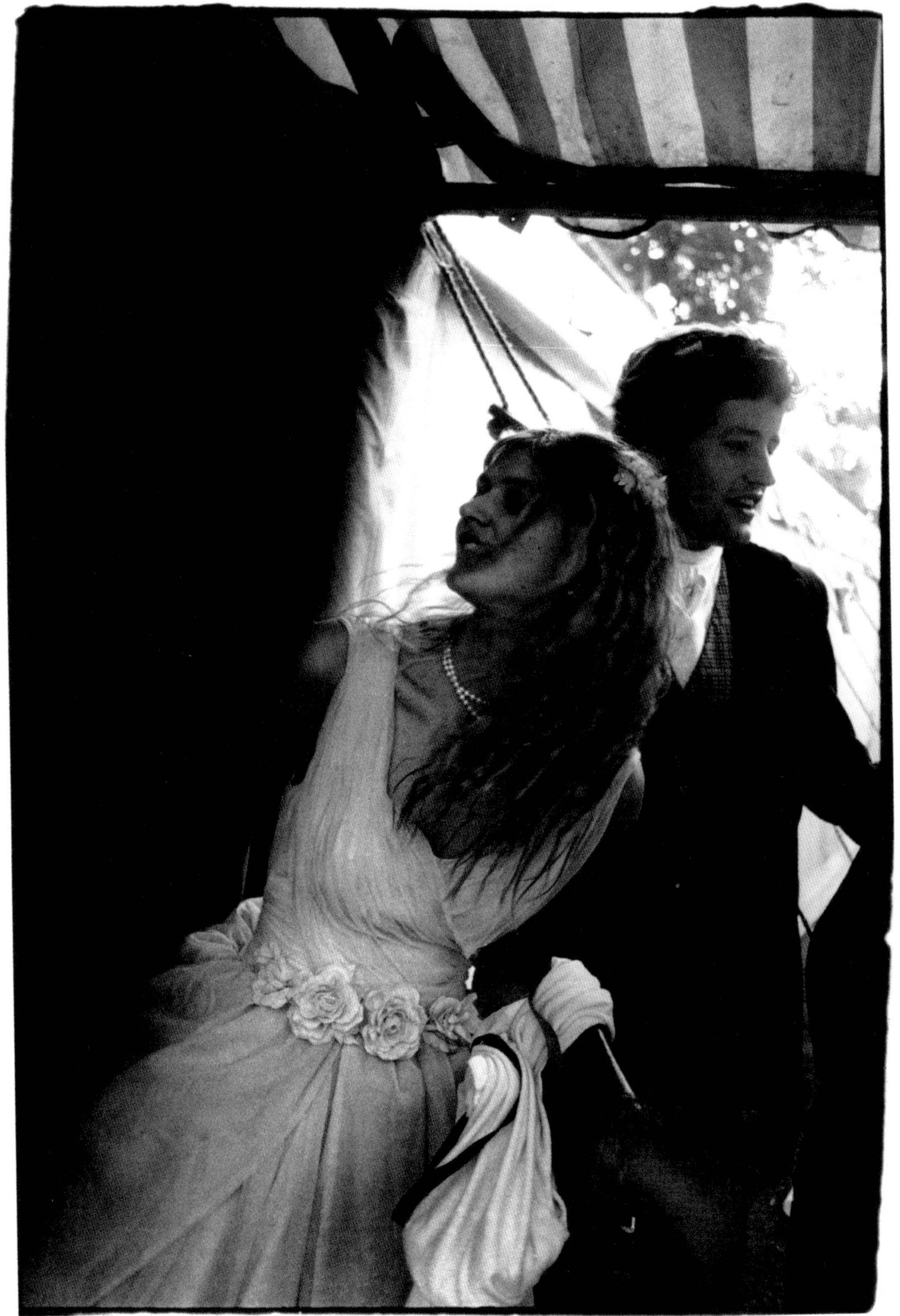

Rachel and Rupert Carnegie during the Magdalene May Ball, 17 June 1981

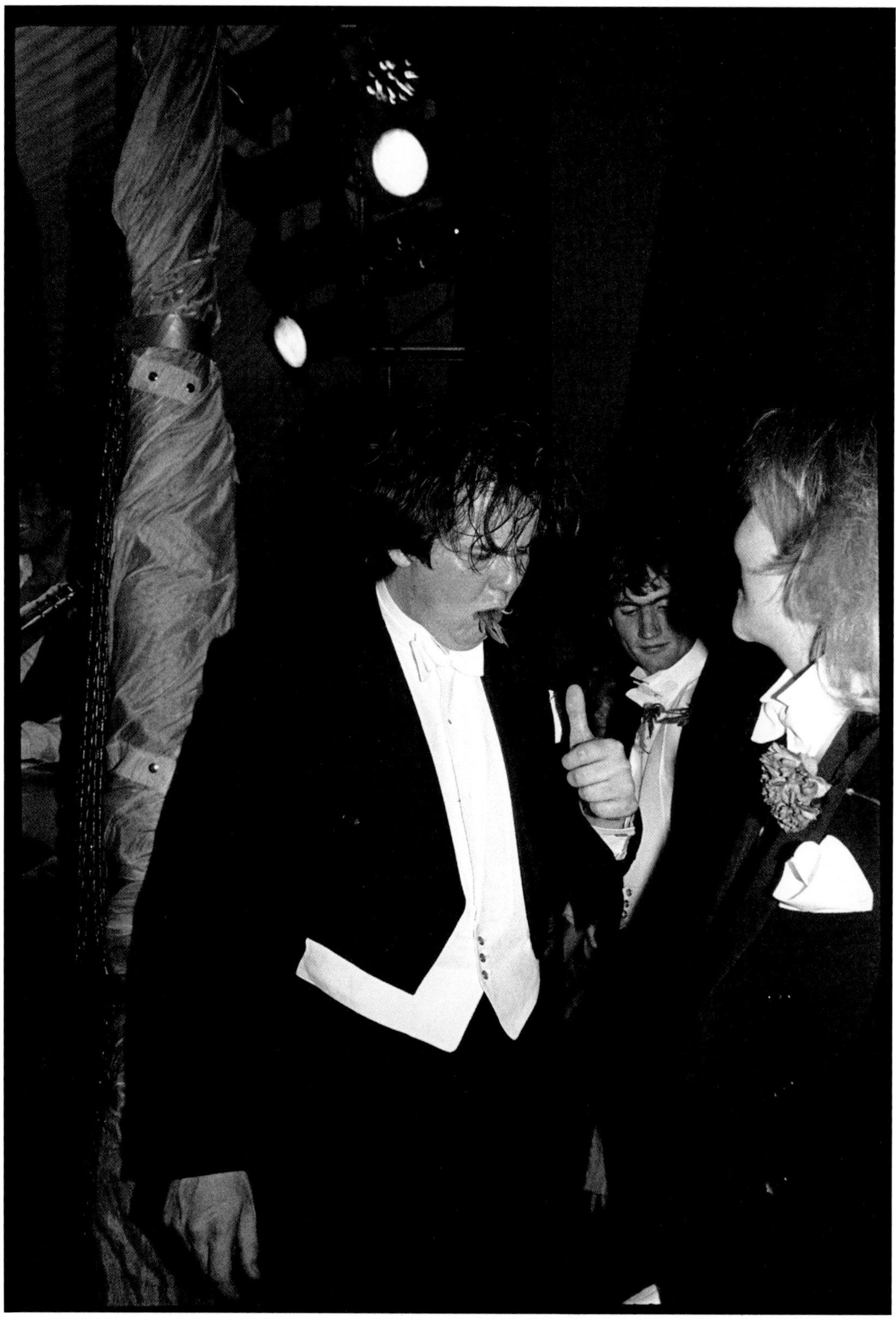

Ed Henry, Magdalene May Ball, 15 June 1983

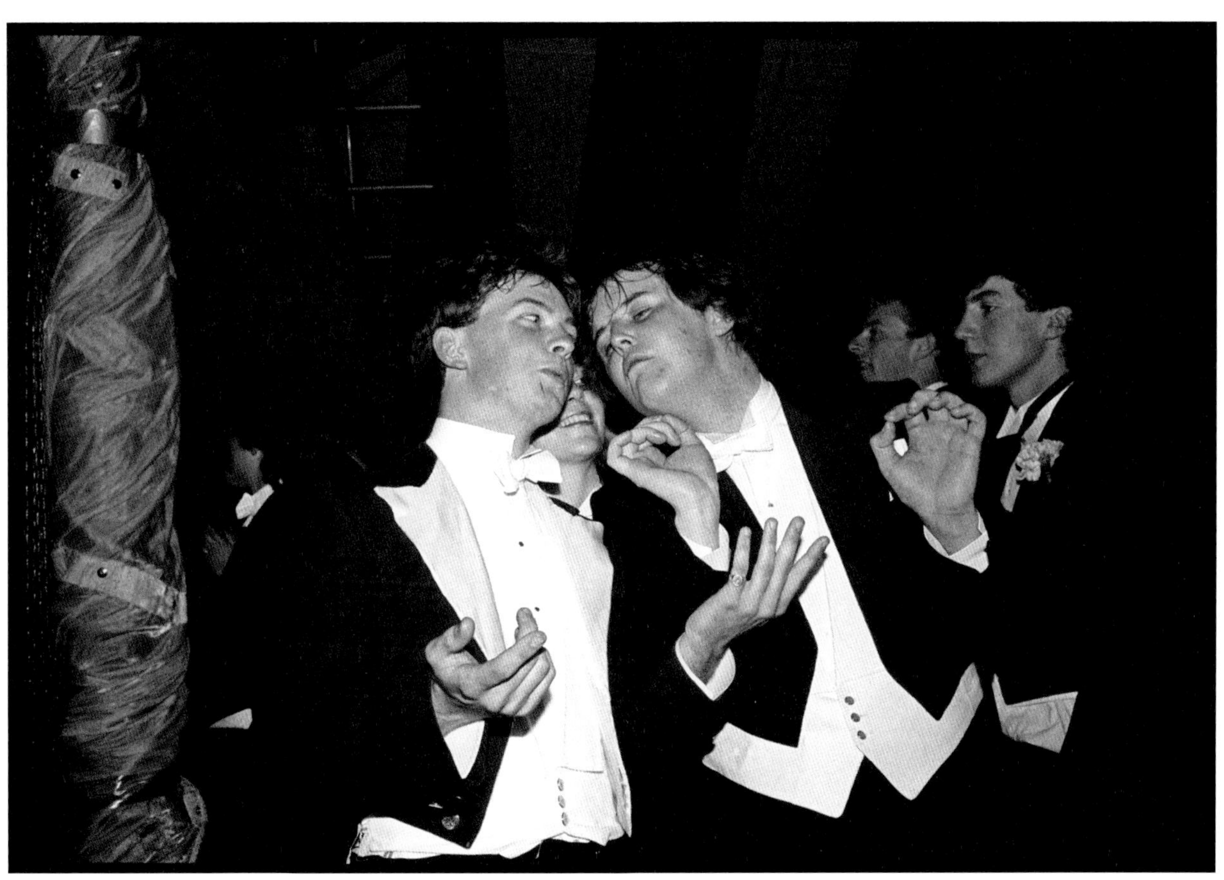

Simon Roberts and Ed Henry, Magdalene May Ball, 15 June 1983

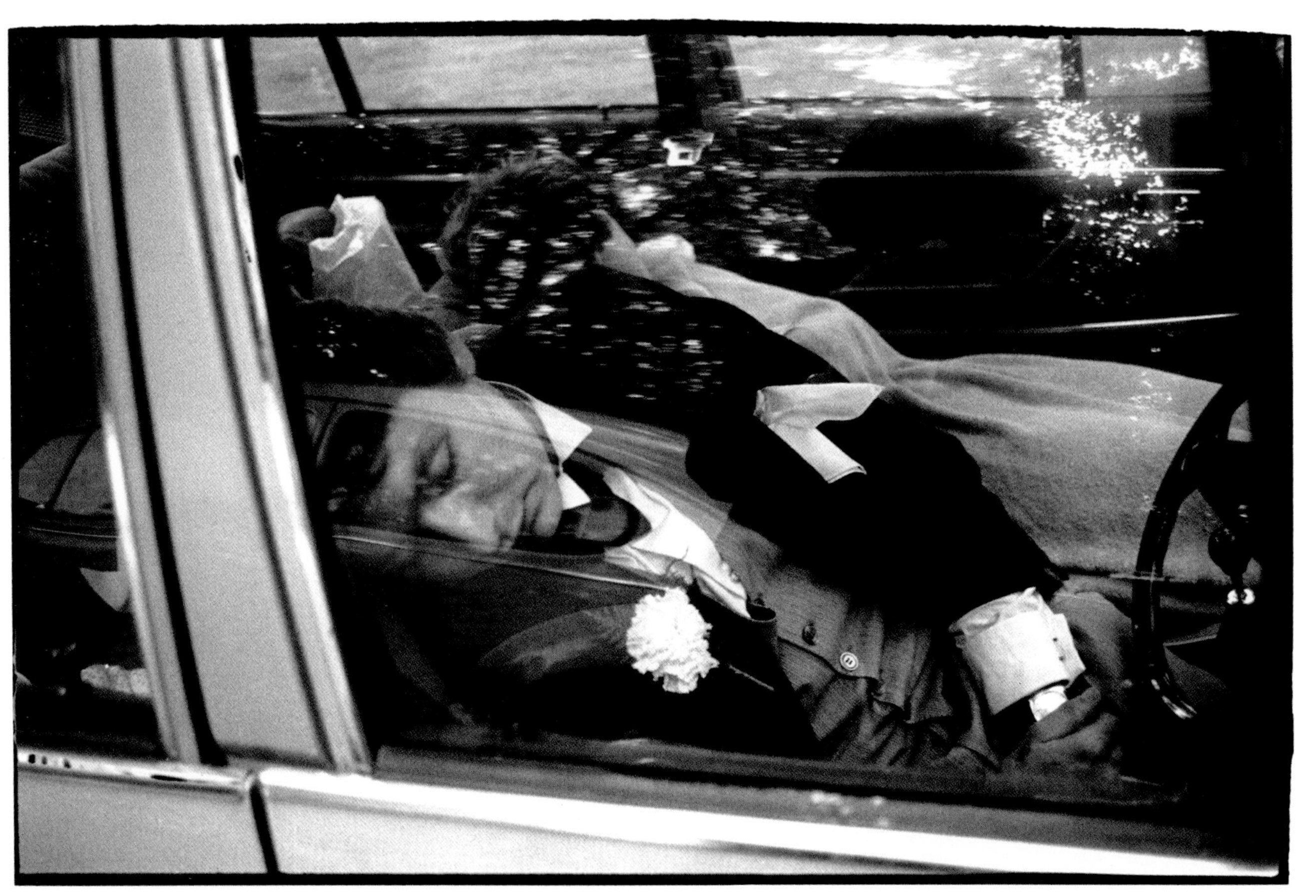

After the Trinity May Ball, 15 June 1981

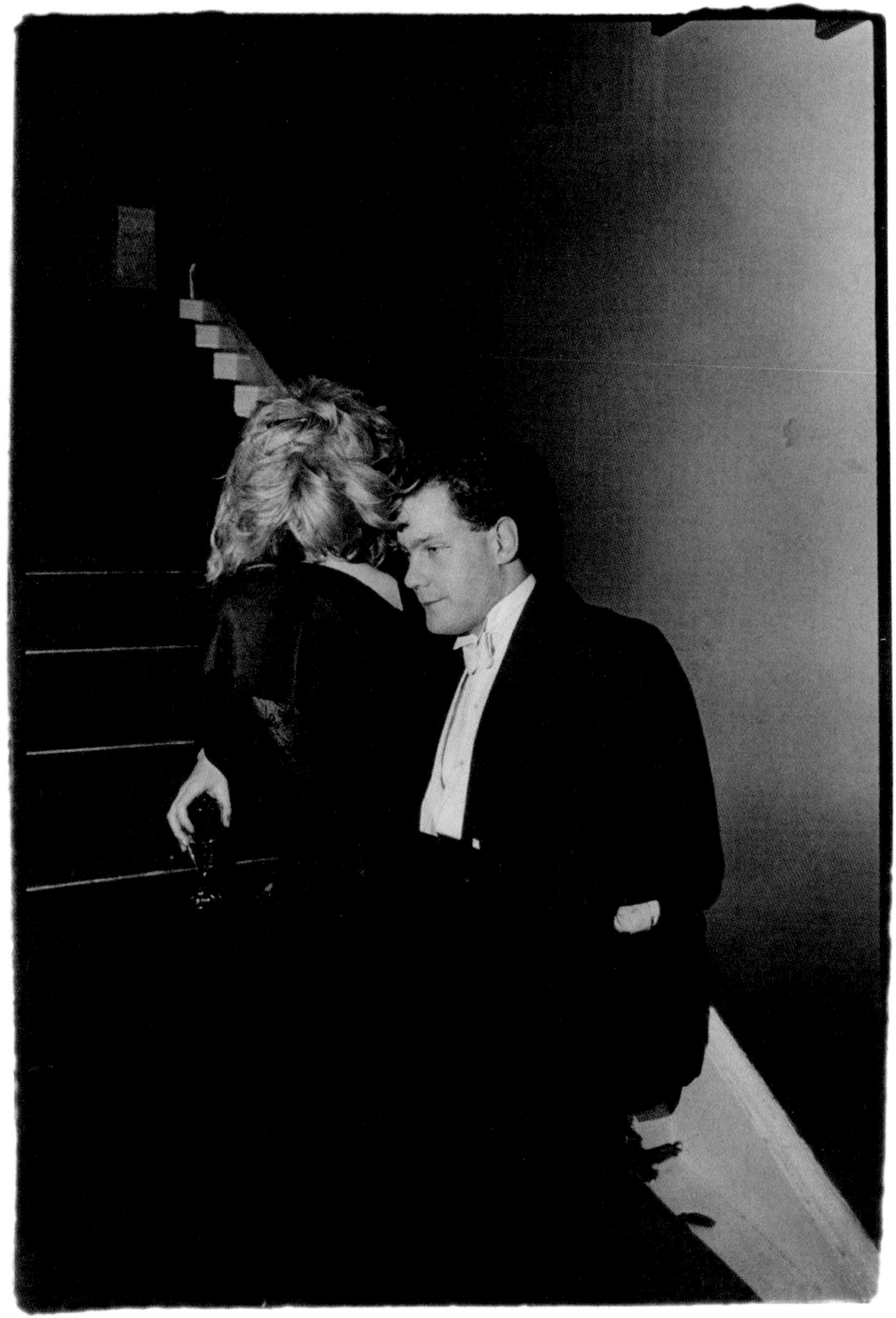

Alexia Althusen and Gus Hochschild, Pitt Club Ball, February 1988

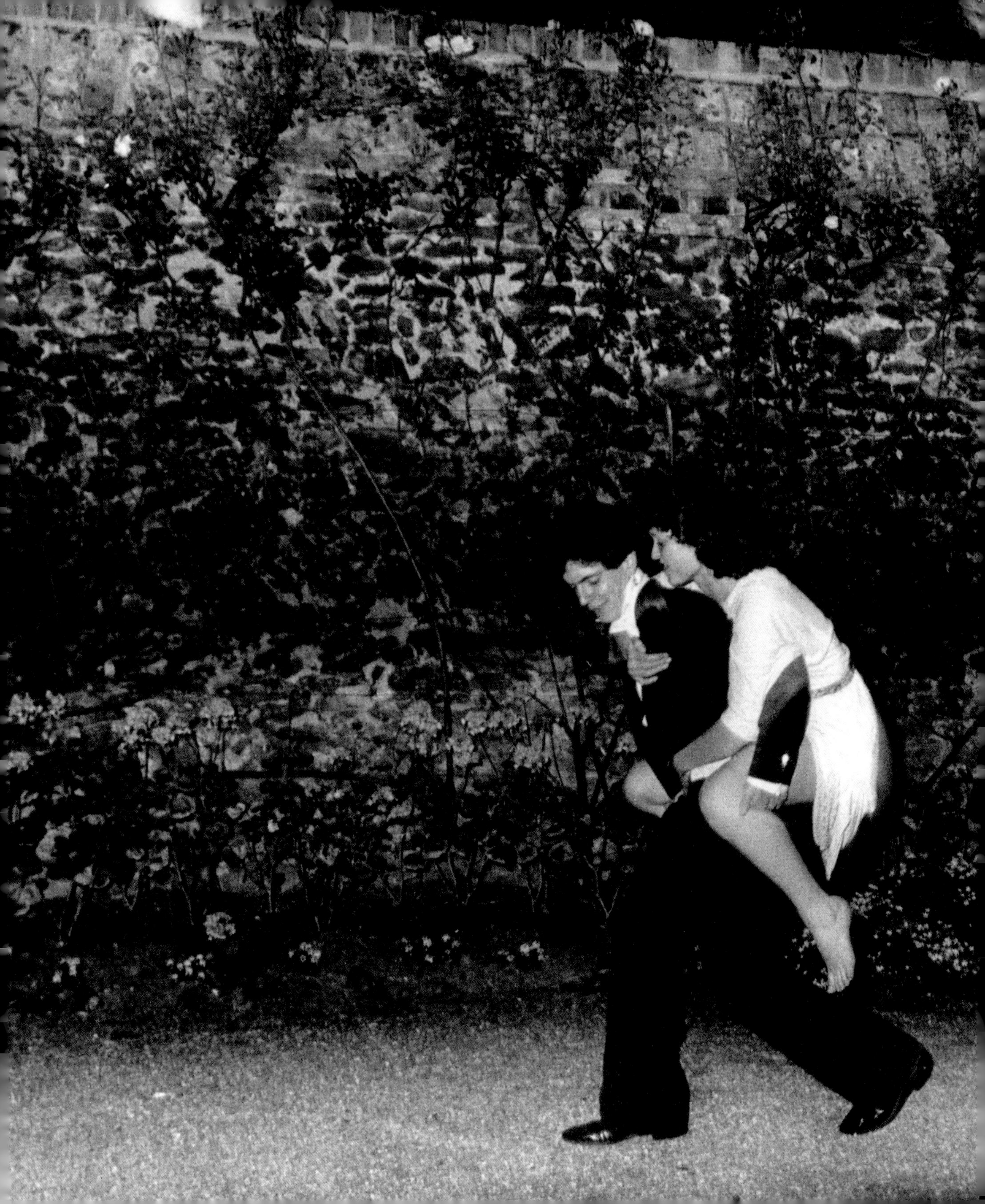

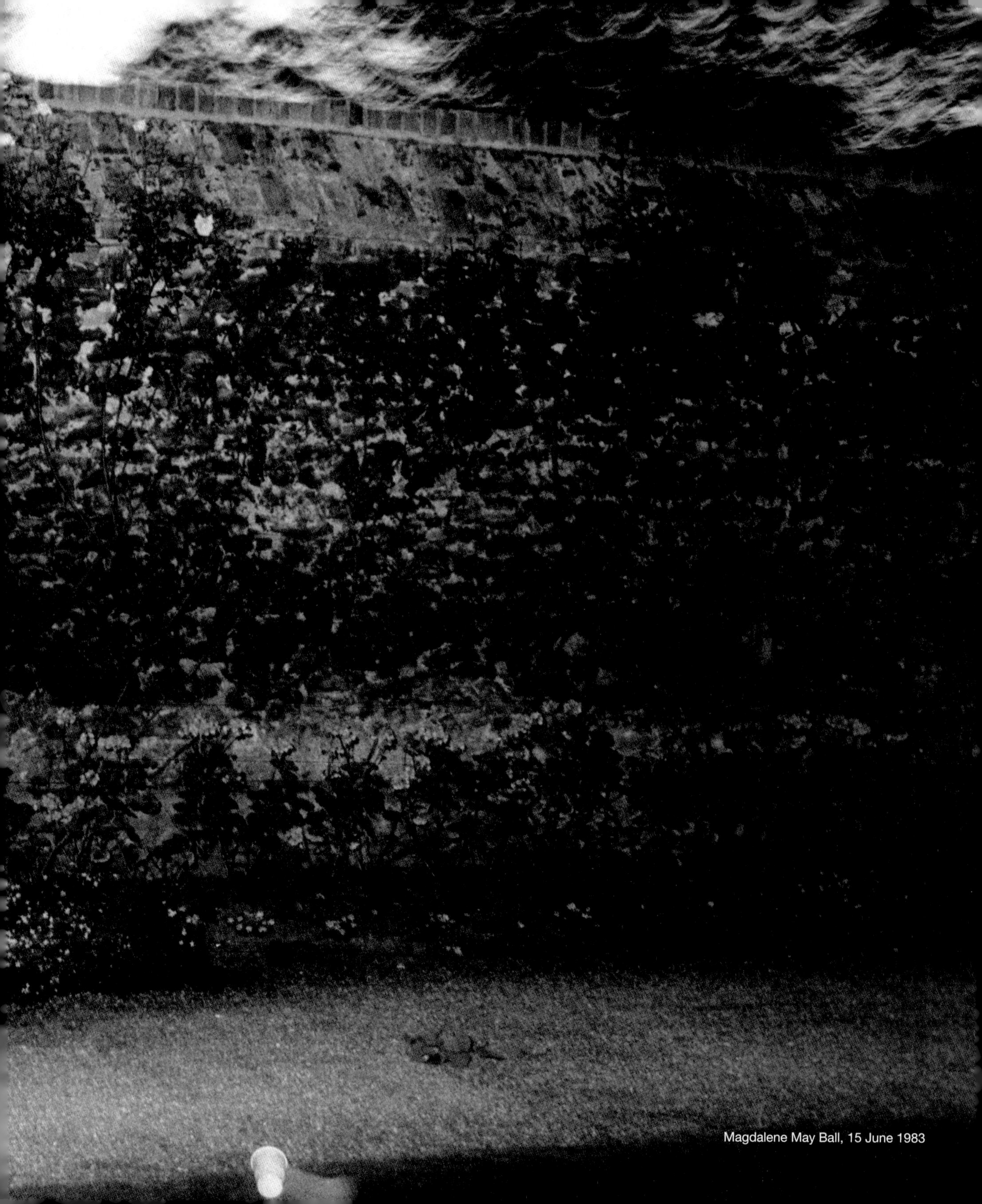

Magdalene May Ball, 15 June 1983

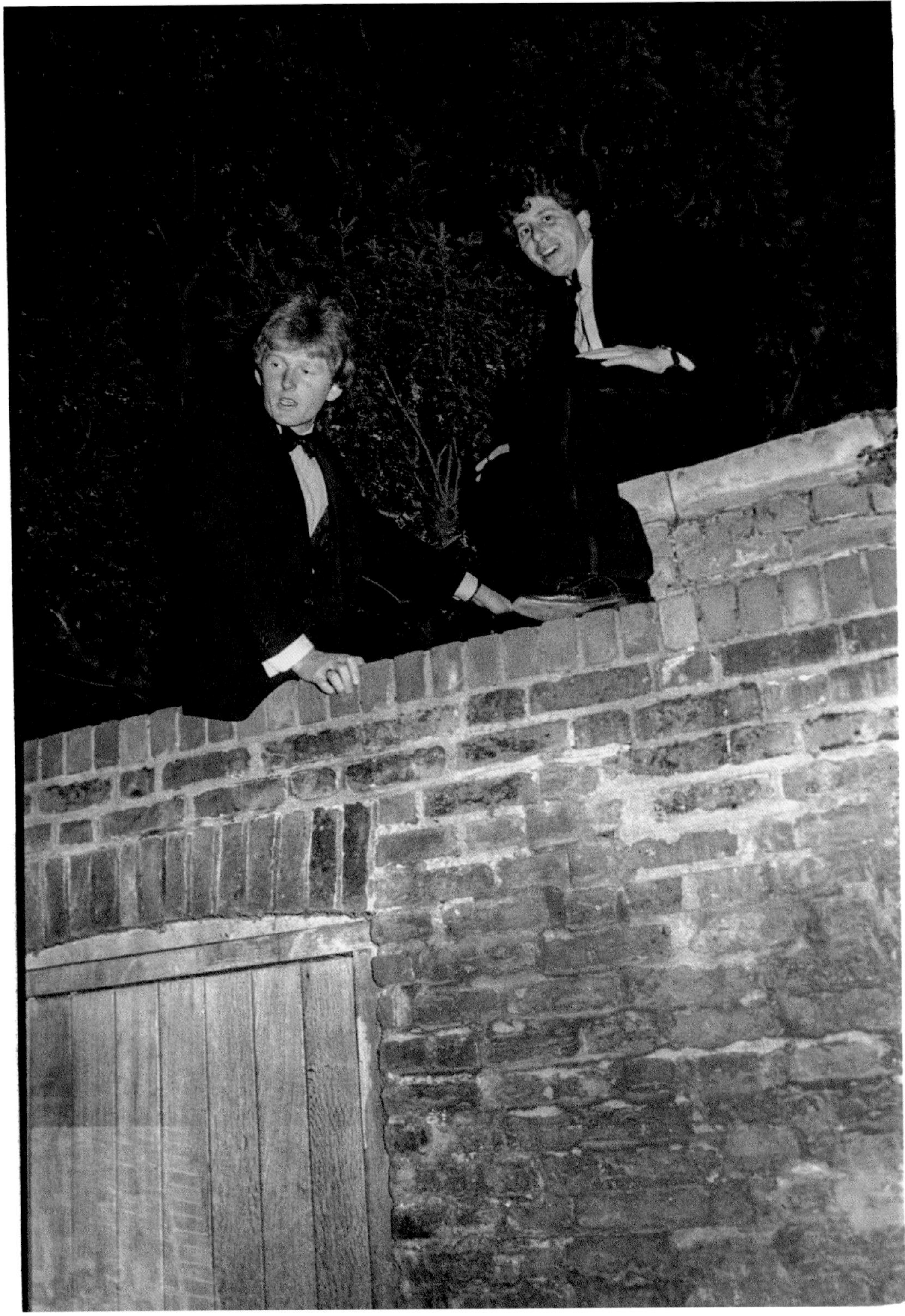

Climbing into the Trinity May Ball, 15 June 1981

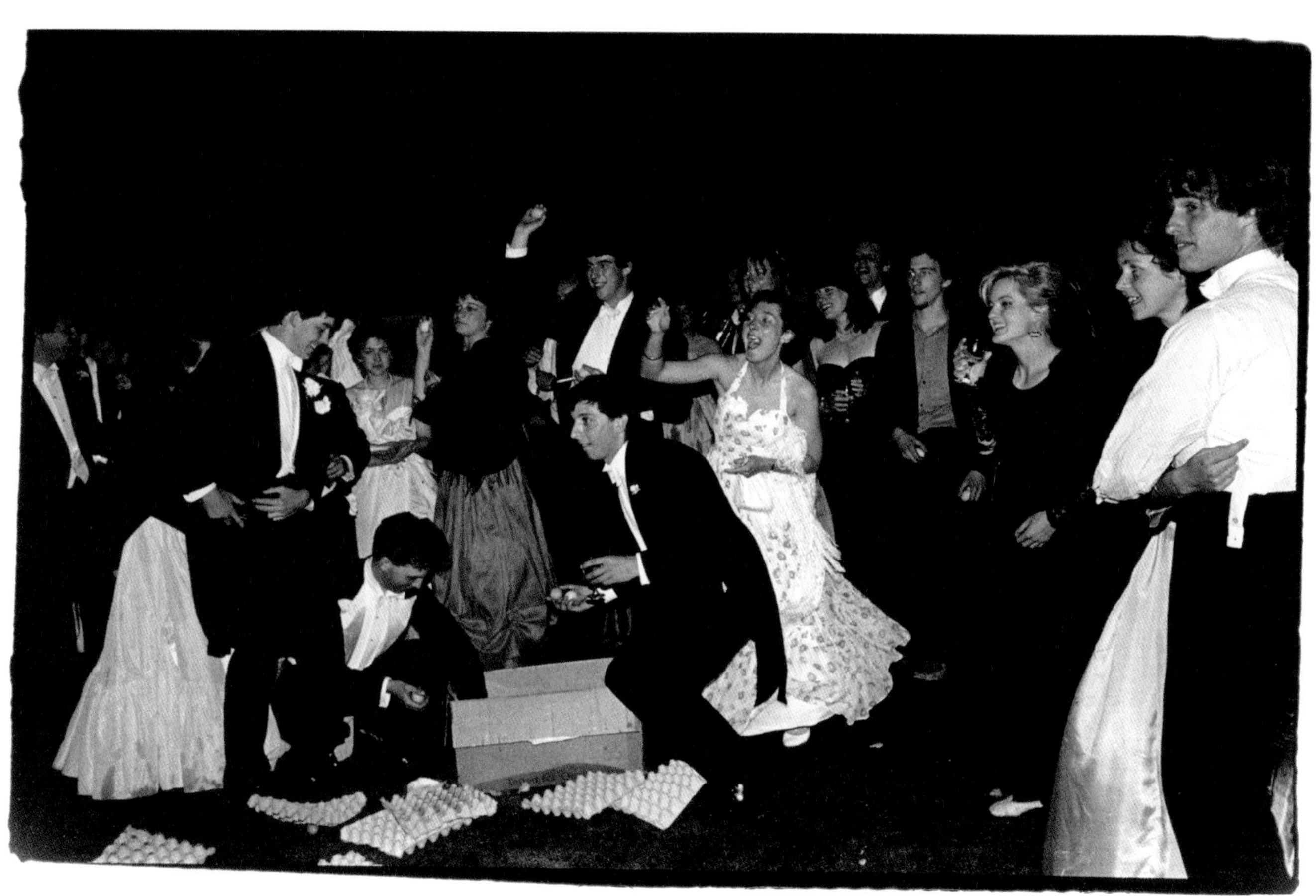

Ball-goers throwing eggs at a gatecrasher in stocks, Magdalene May Ball, 15 June 1983

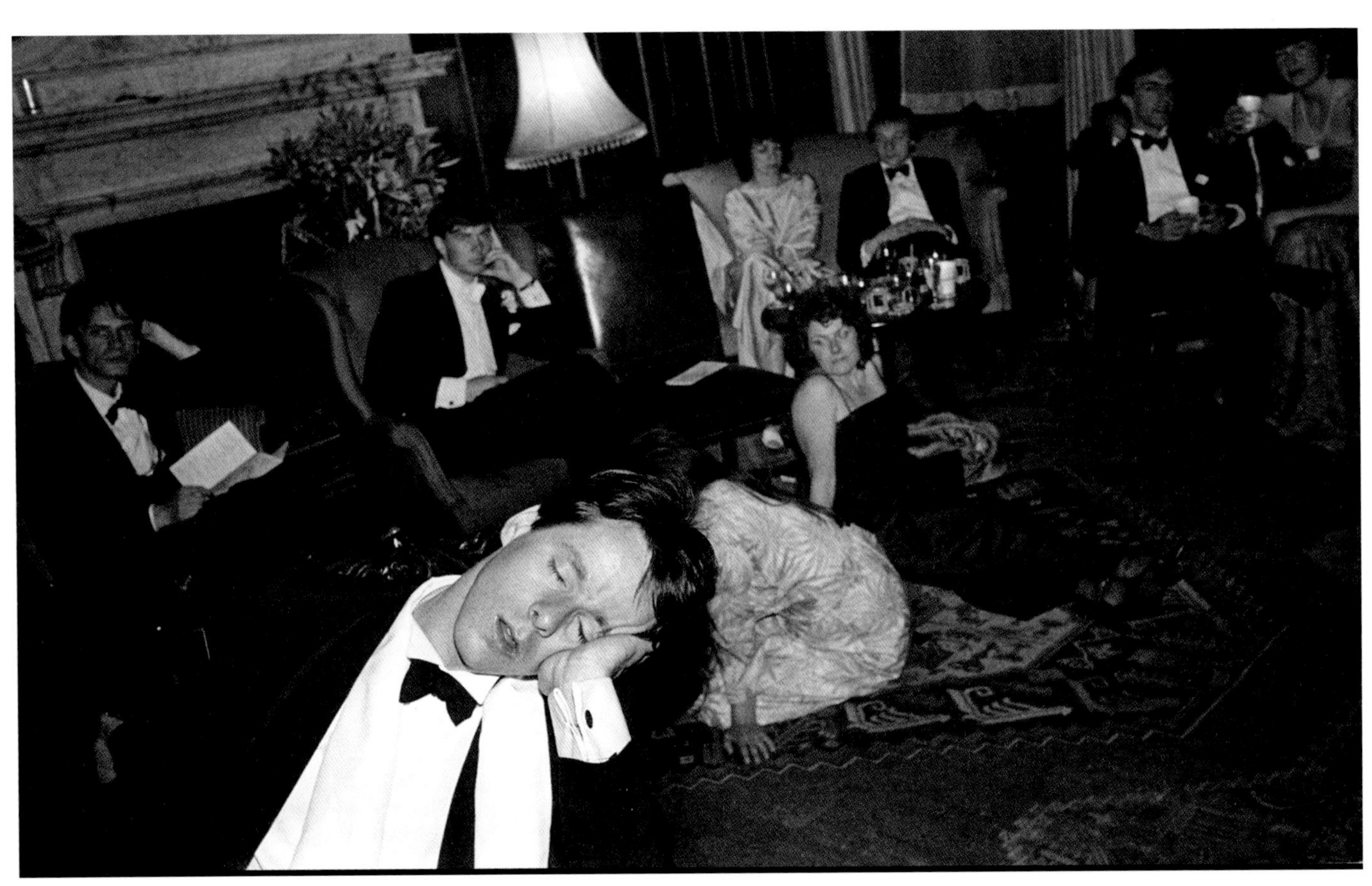

Trinity Hall May Ball, 1983

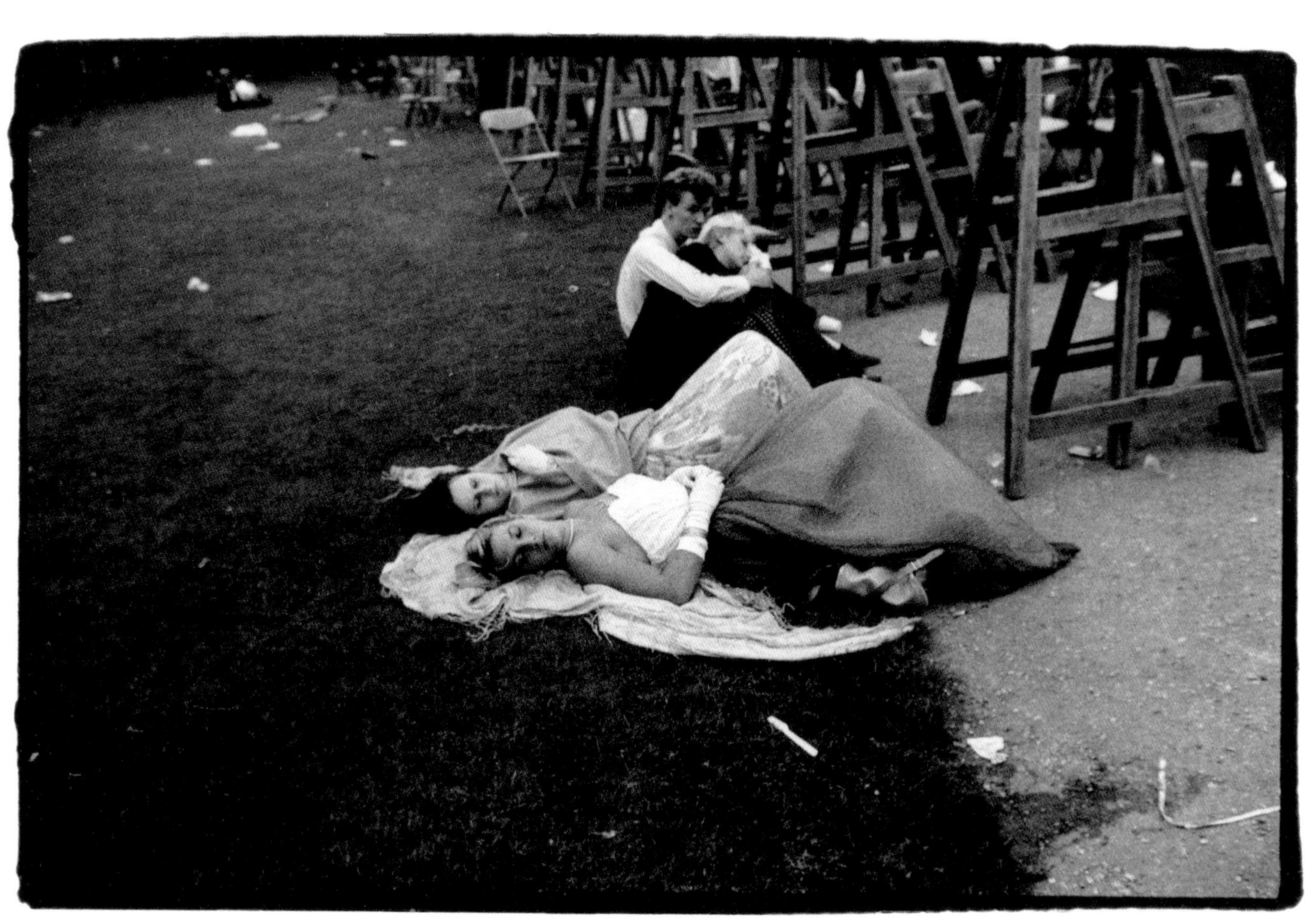

6 a.m., Trinity May Ball, 18 June 1984

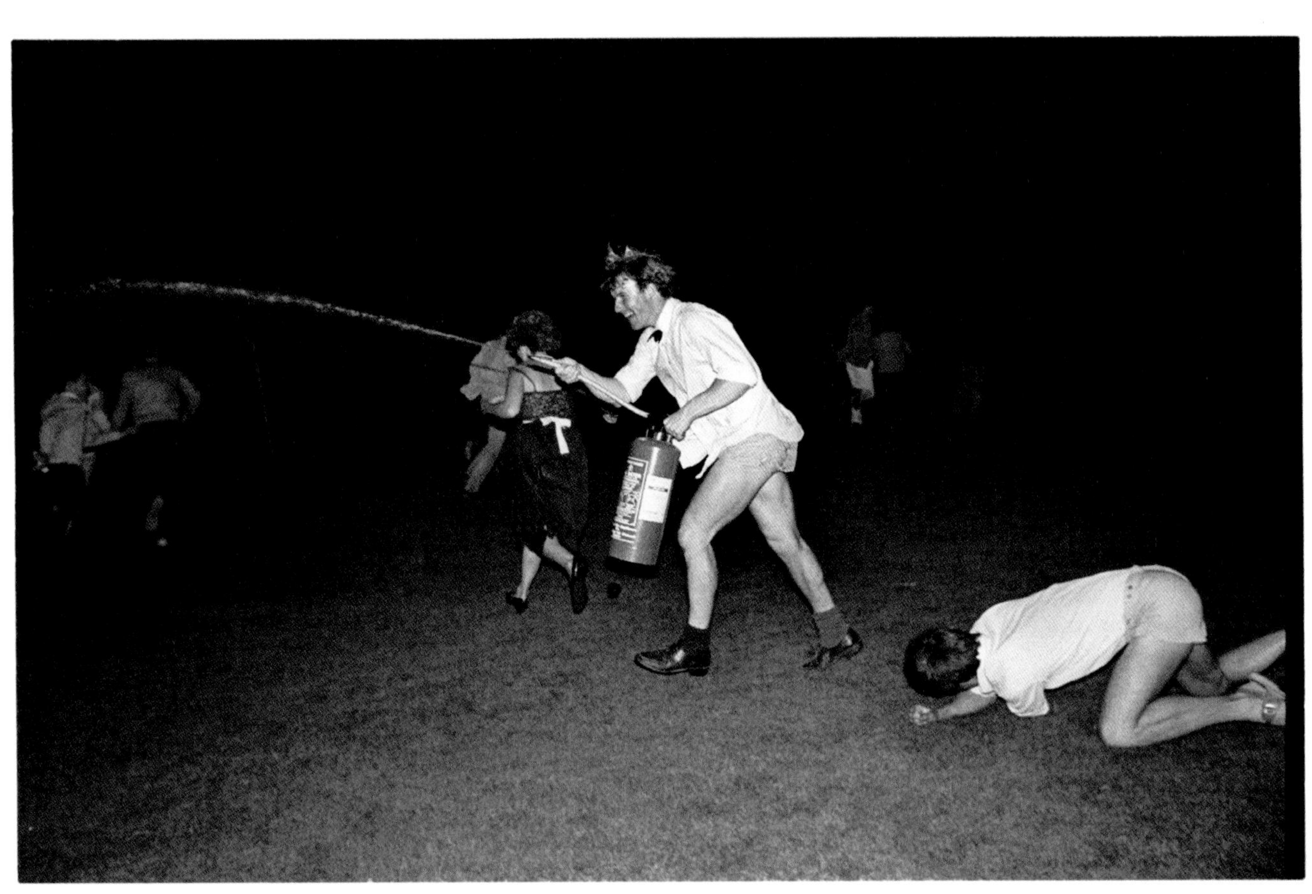

Burning Boats, Downing College, June 1984

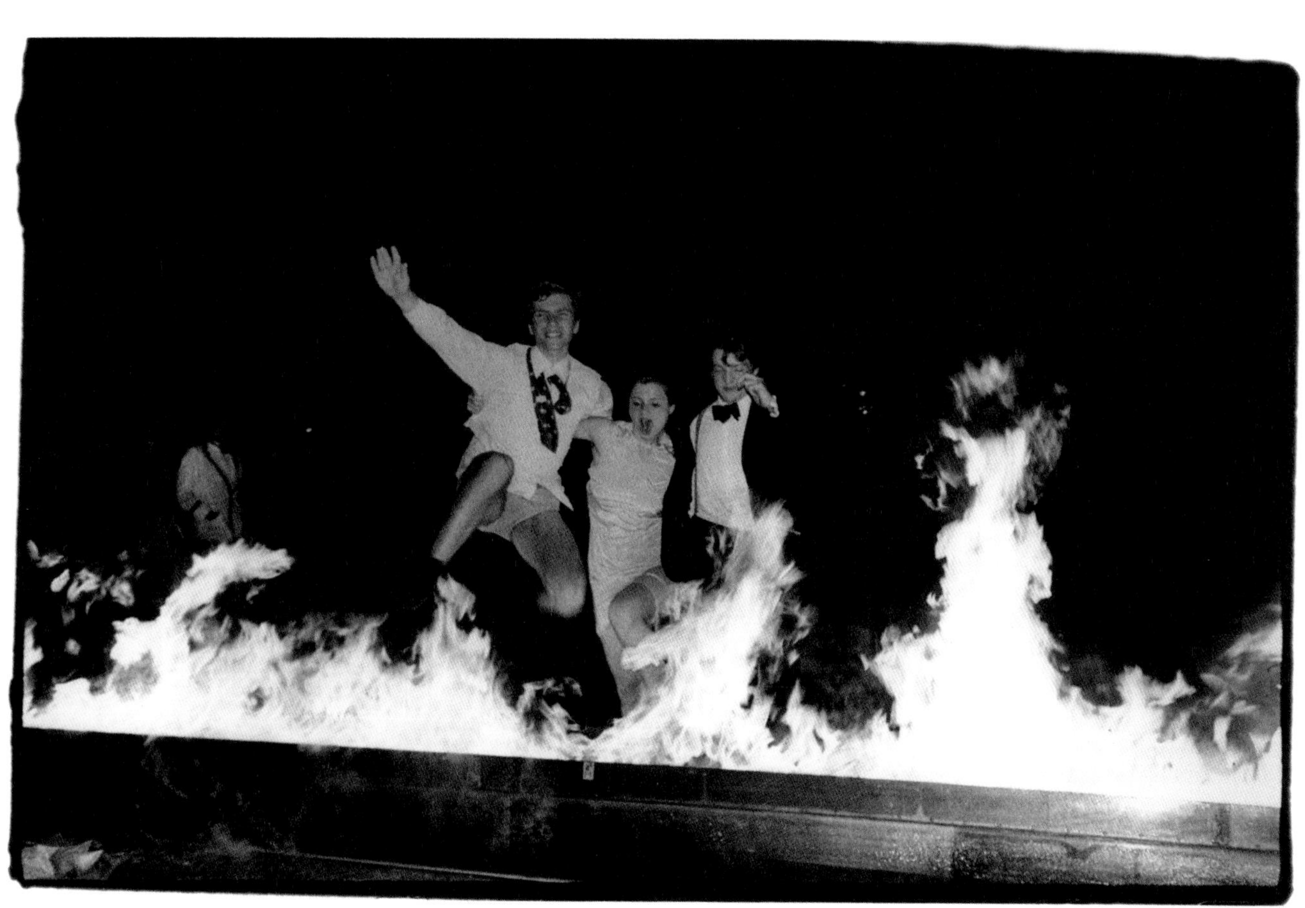

Burning Boats, Downing College, June 1984

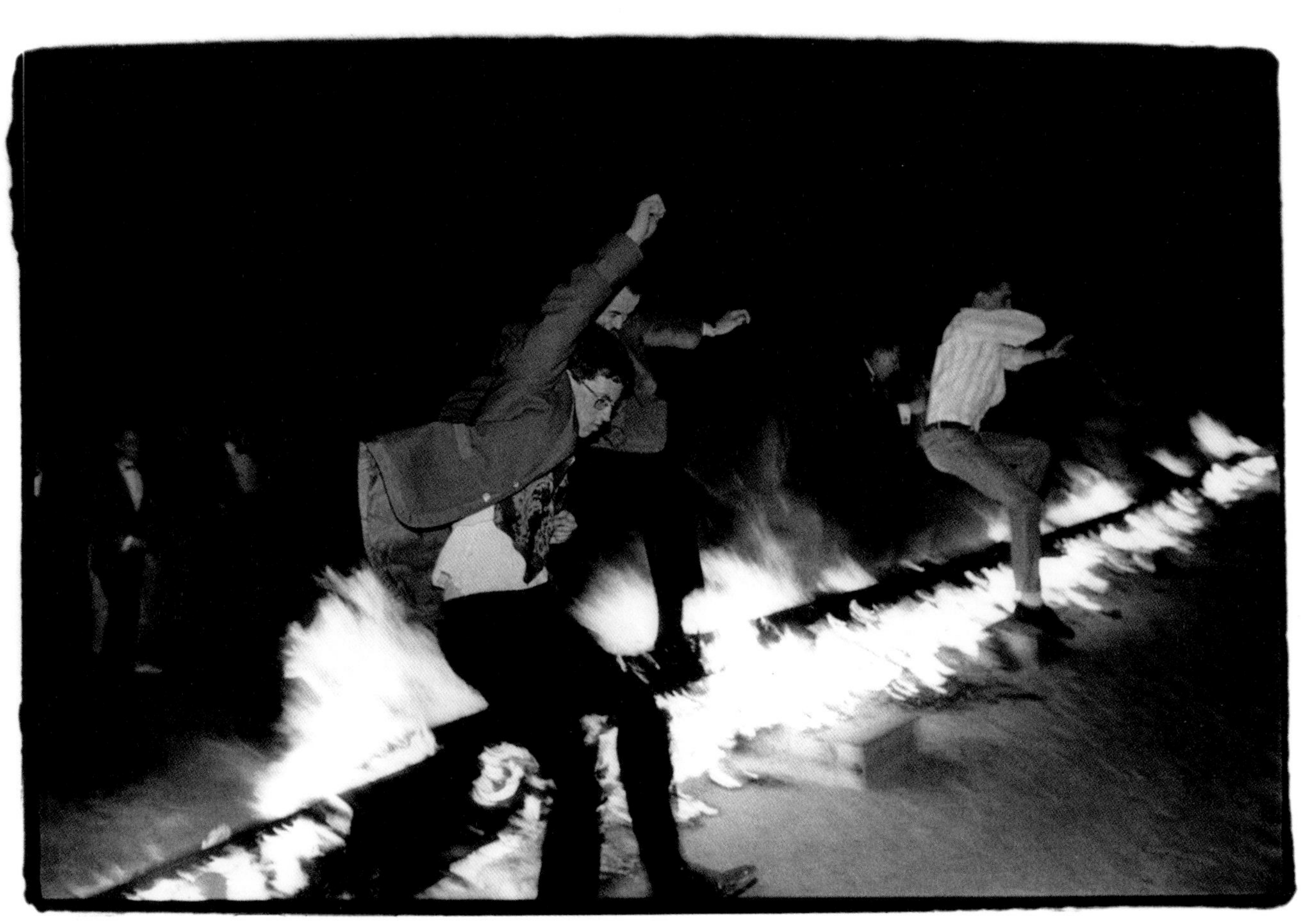

Burning Boats, St John's College, June 1988

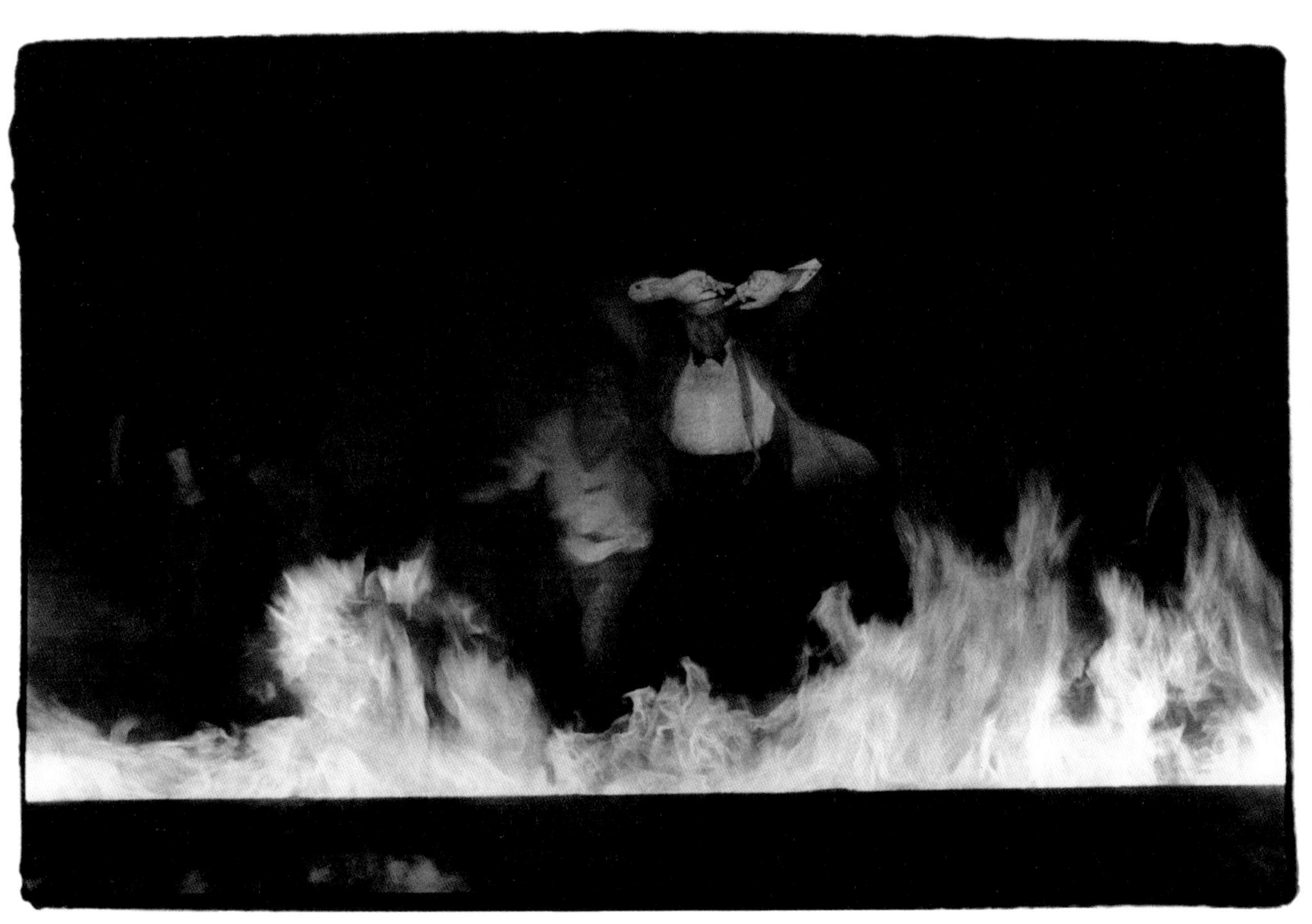

Burning Boats, St John's College, June 1988

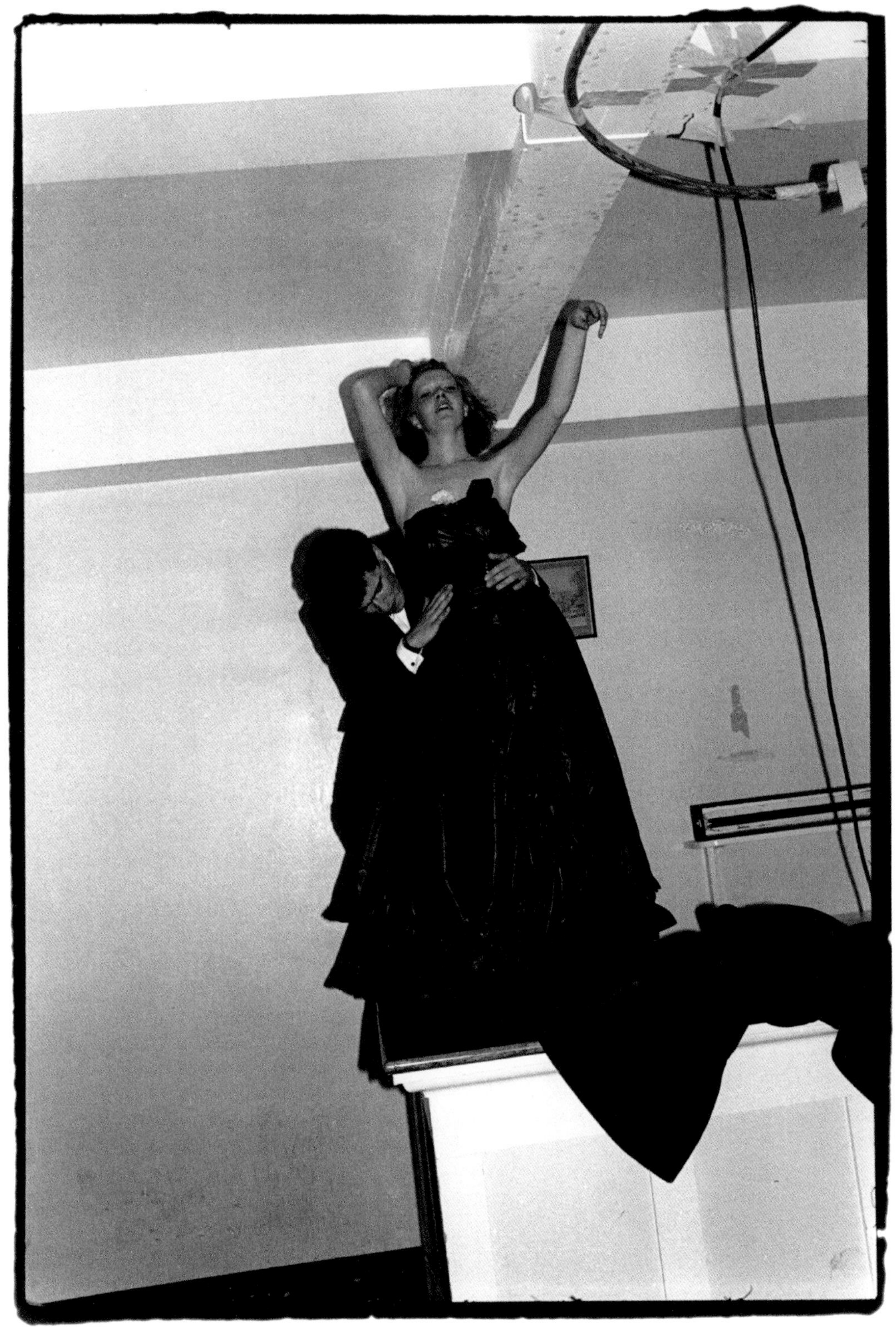

Ralph Brody and Sarah Charles, Pitt Club 150th Anniversary Ball, Newmarket Racecourse, 22 February 1983

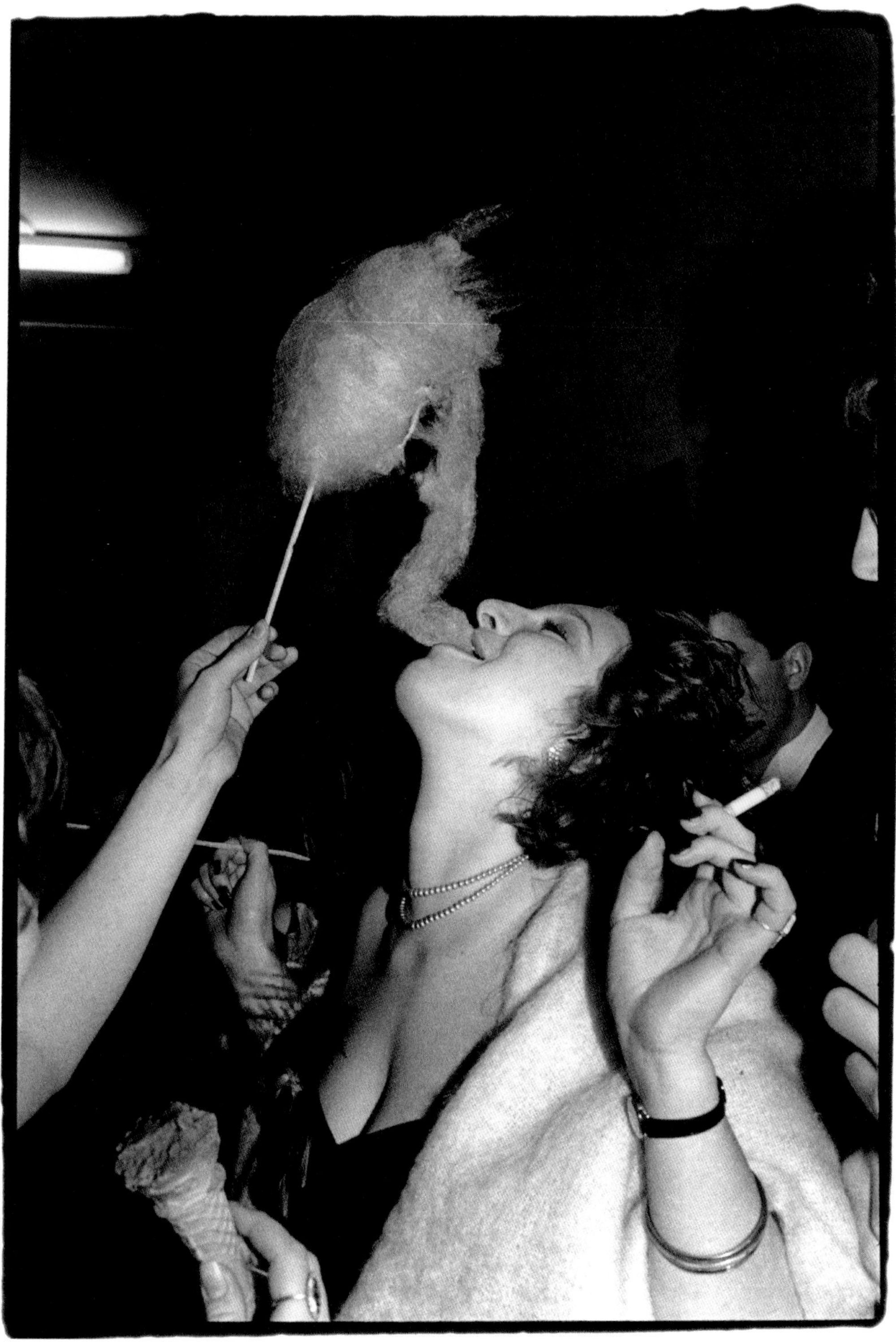

Elizabeth Pulford being fed candyfloss, Cambridge University Charity Ball, Guildhall, 1985

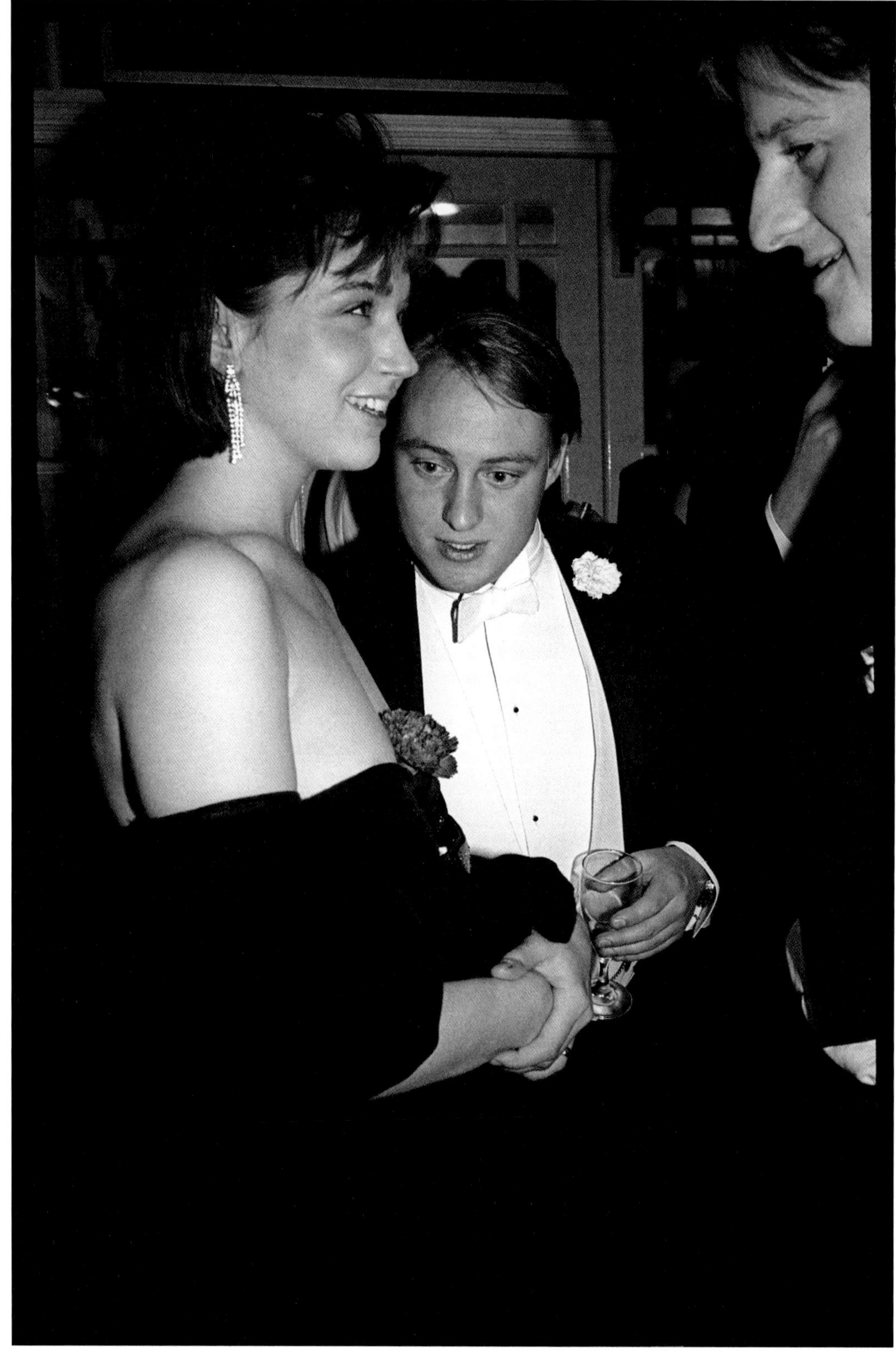

Andrew Roberts, Cambridge University Polo Club Ball, Newmarket, 22 February 1986

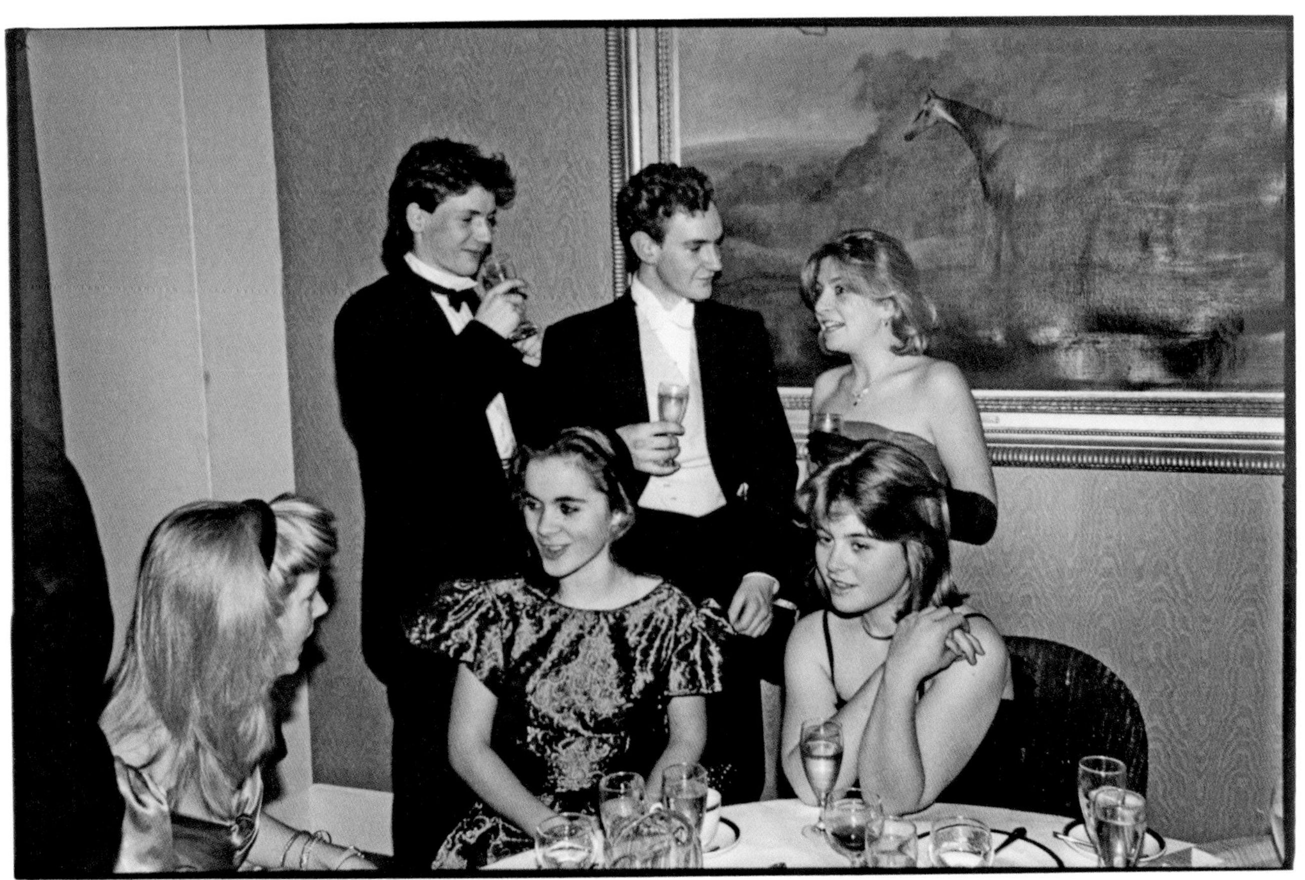

Ben Gladstone, Dominic Armstrong, Laura Keep, Nicola Ogilvy Watson, Christina Traill and Clare Abberton,
Cambridge University Polo Club Ball, Newmarket, 22 February 1986

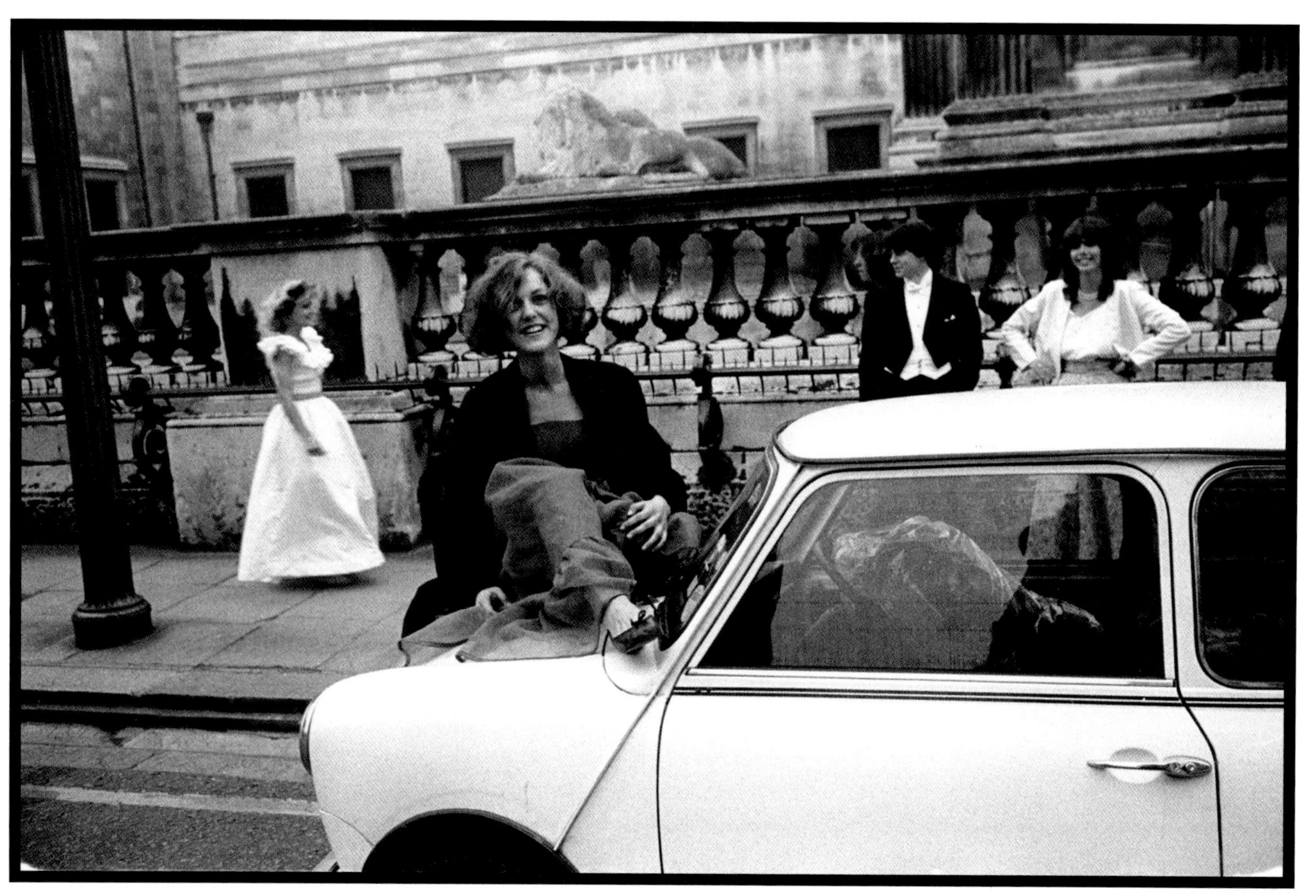

Georgia de Chamberat early in the morning after a May Ball, 18 June 1984

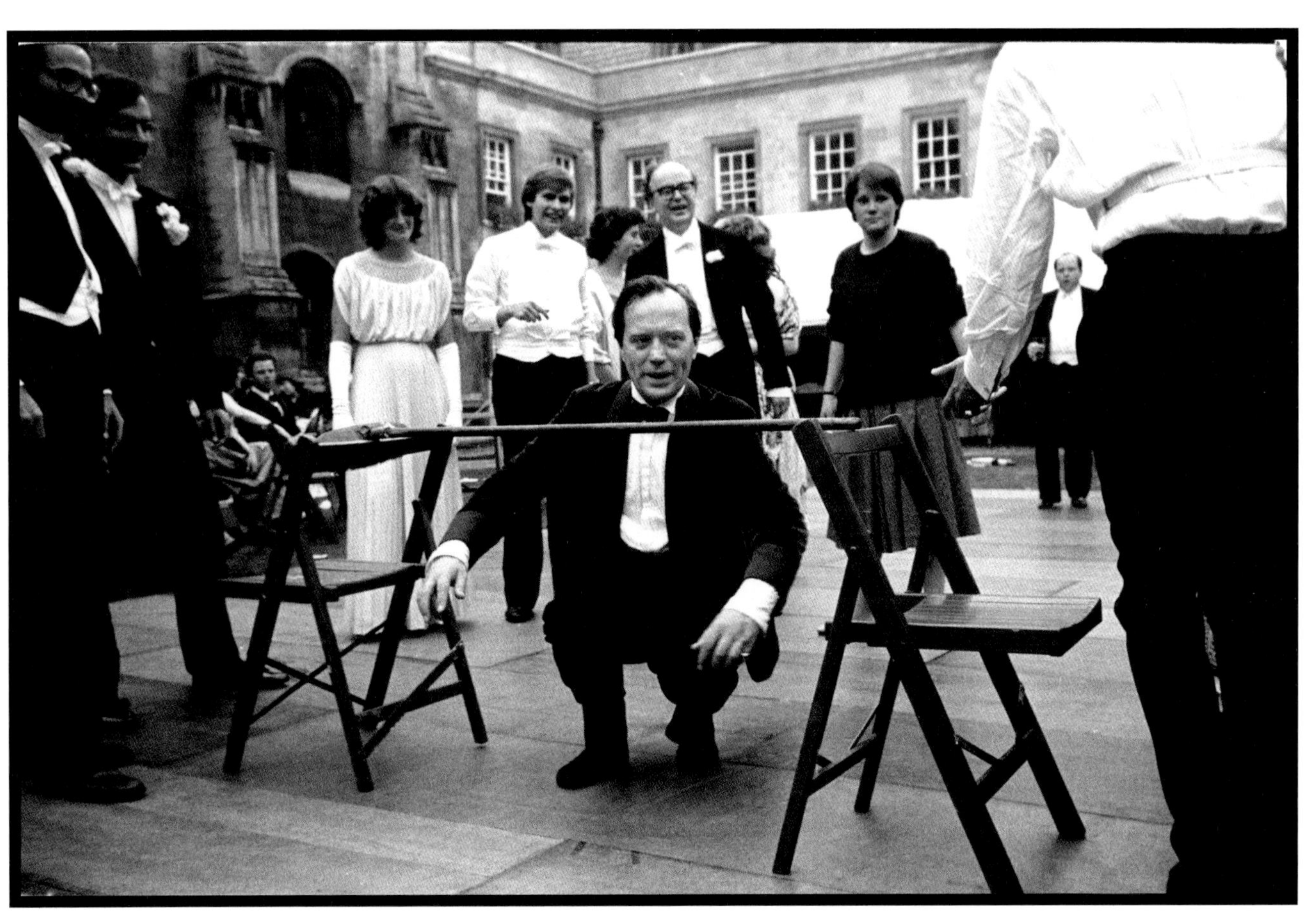

Nicholas Corriman dancing during the Peterhouse 7th Centenary Ball, 1984

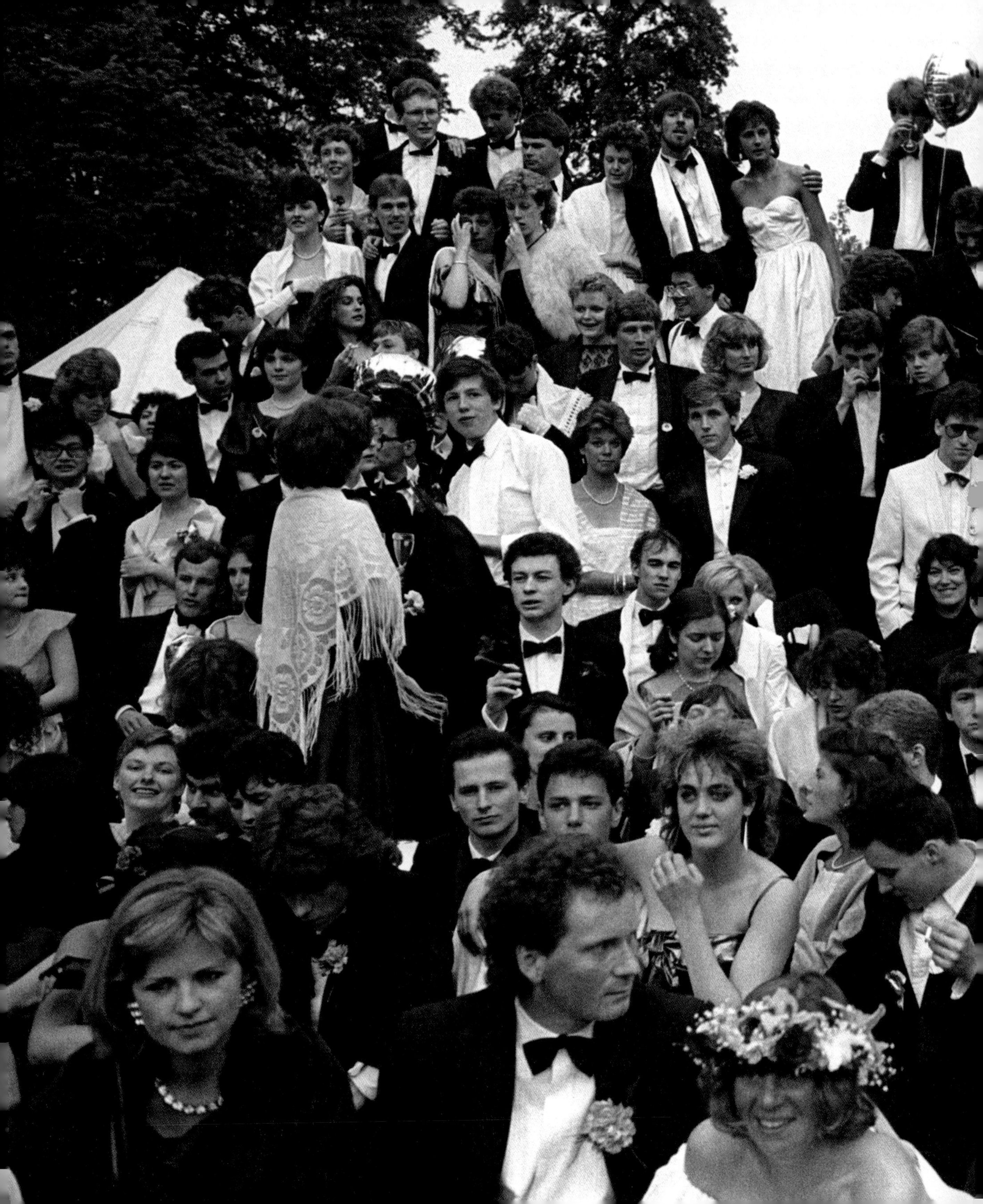

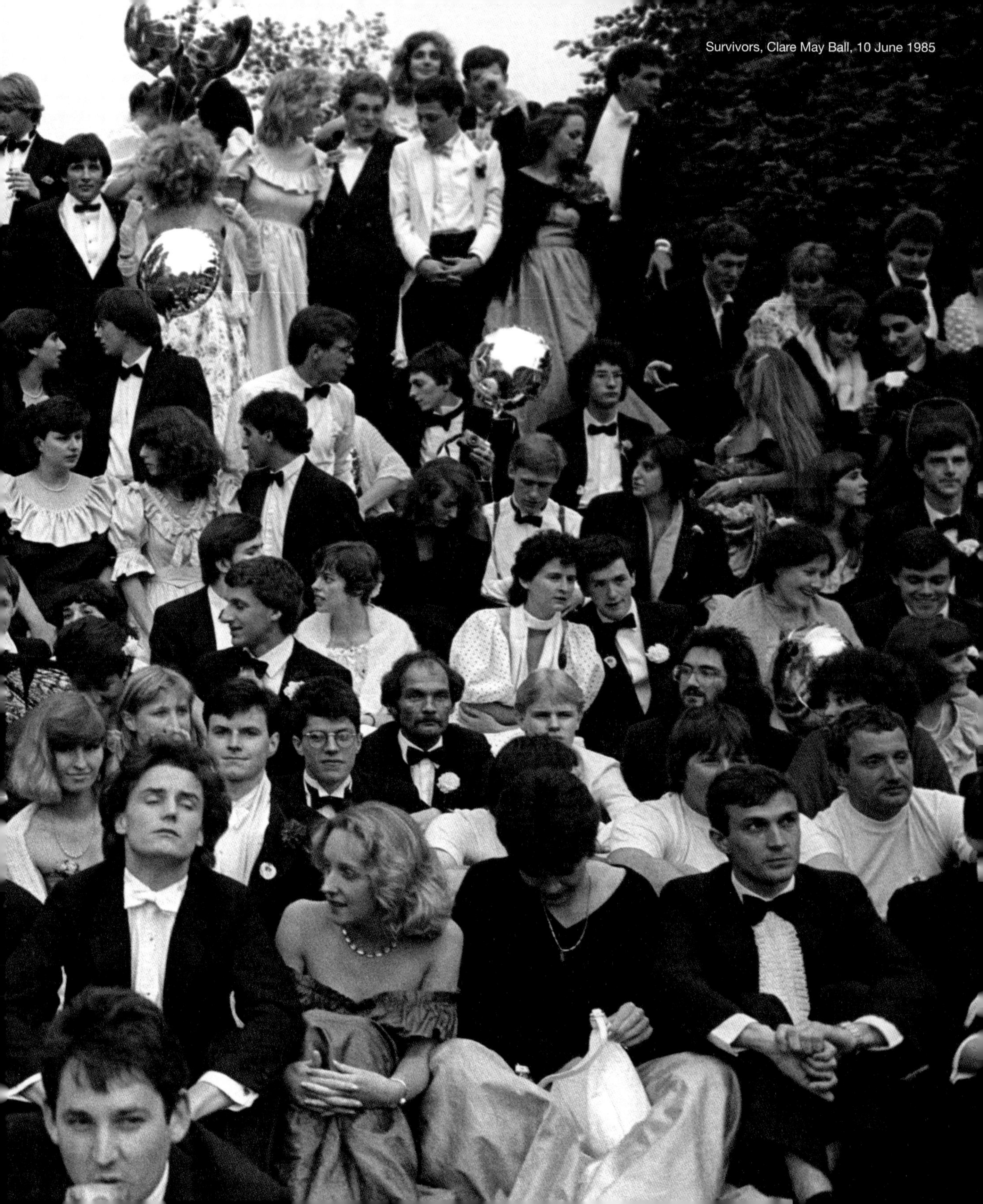

Survivors, Clare May Ball, 10 June 1985

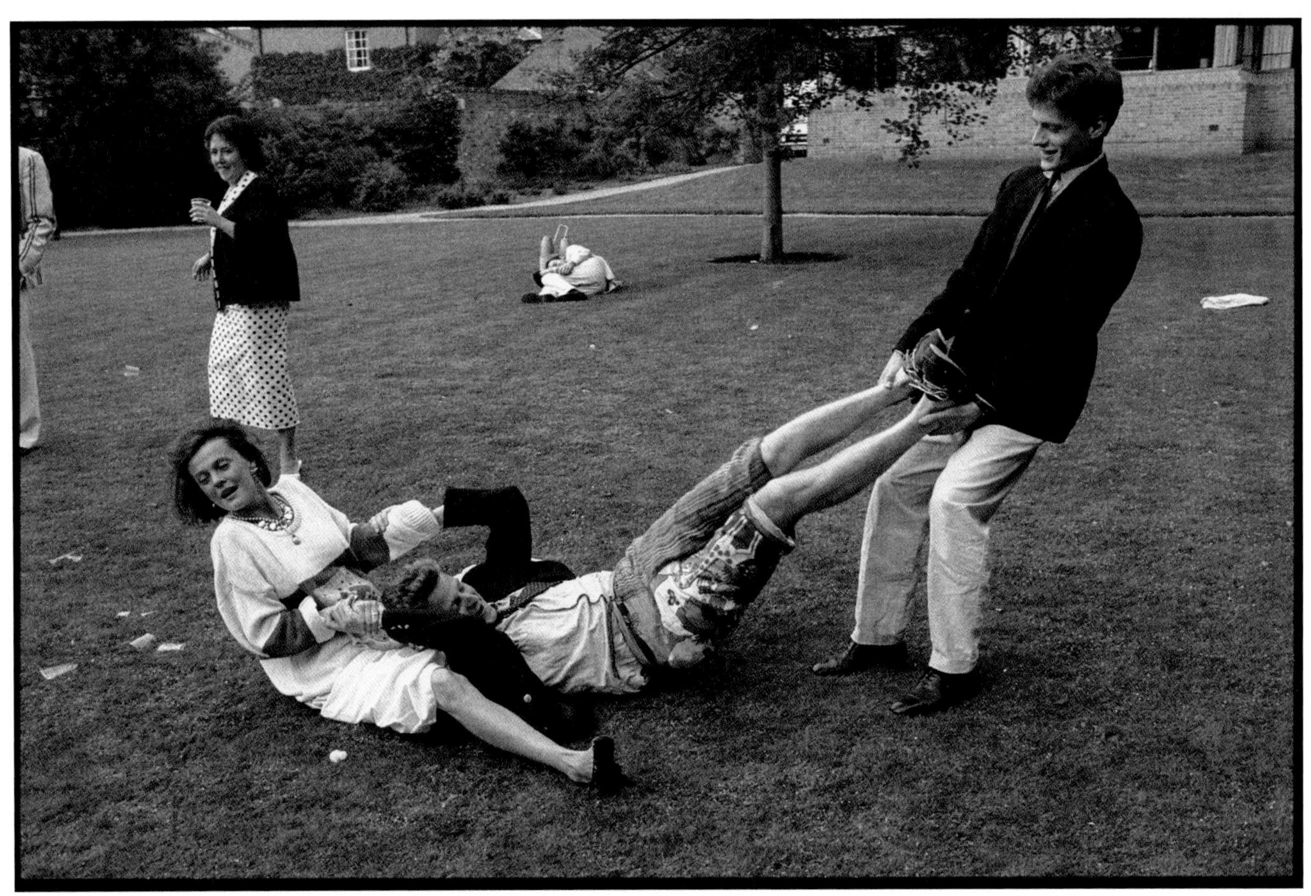

Drinks, Peterhouse Scholars Garden, June 1986

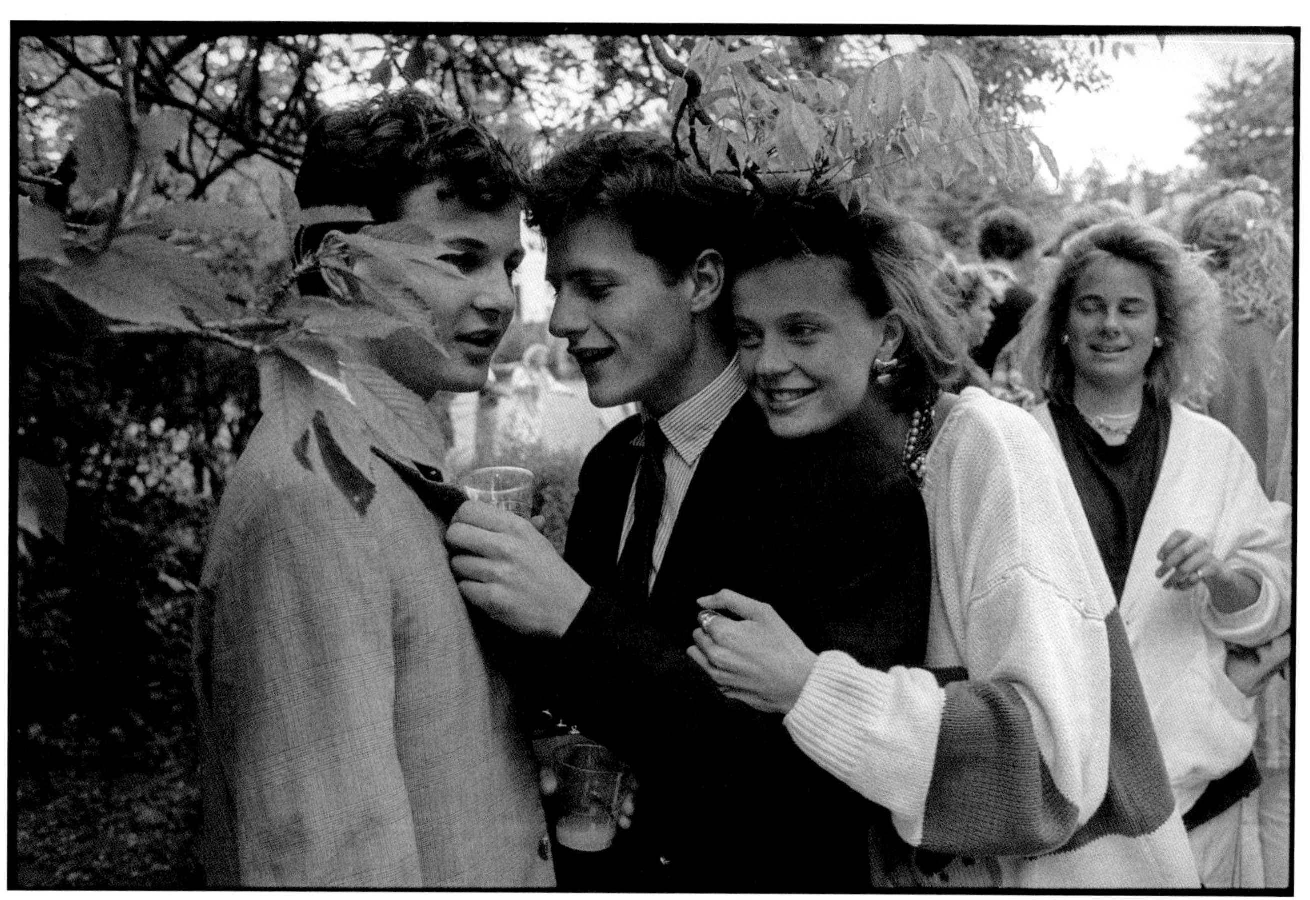

Drinks, Peterhouse Scholars Garden, June 1986

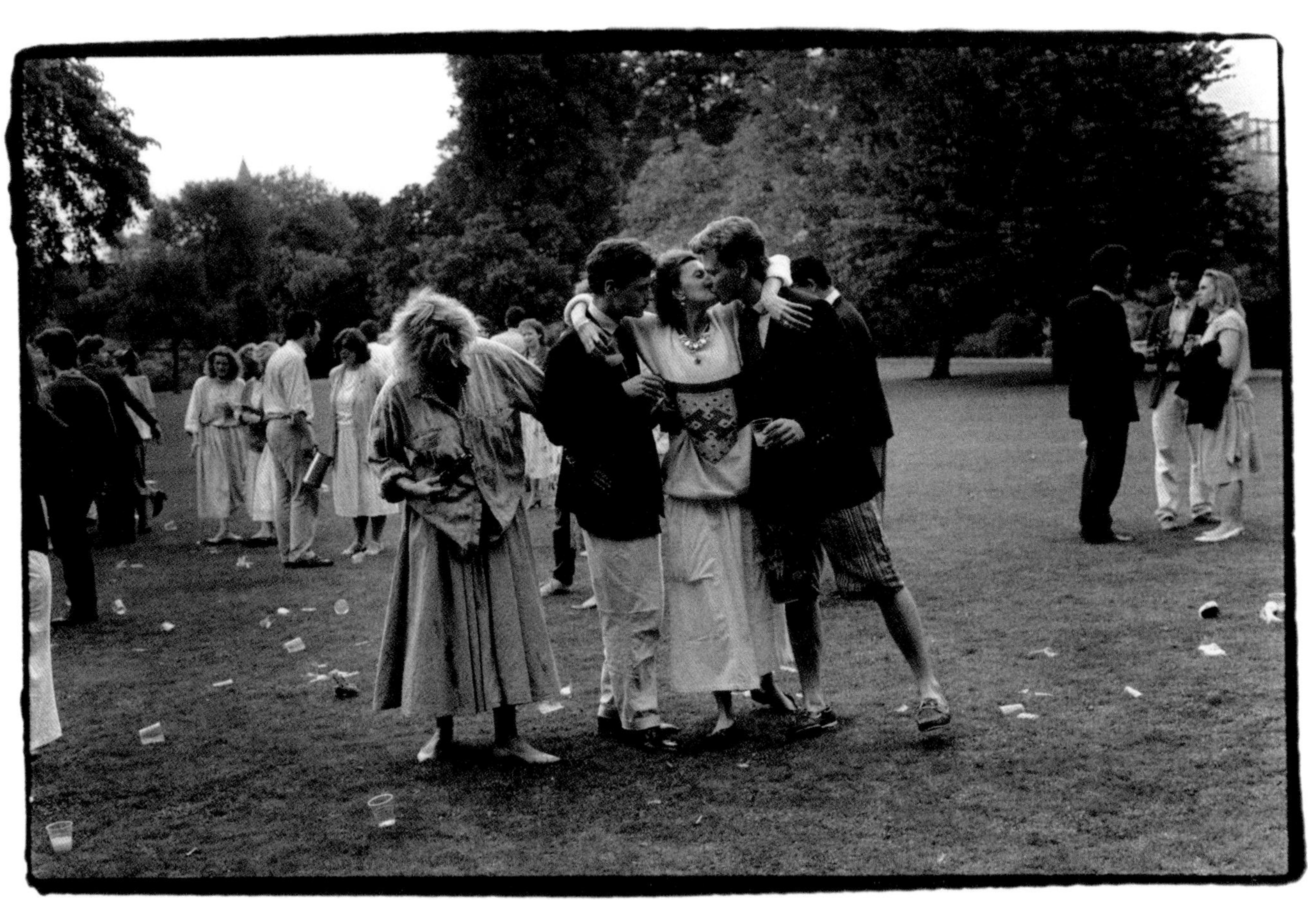

Drinks, Peterhouse Scholars Garden, June 1986

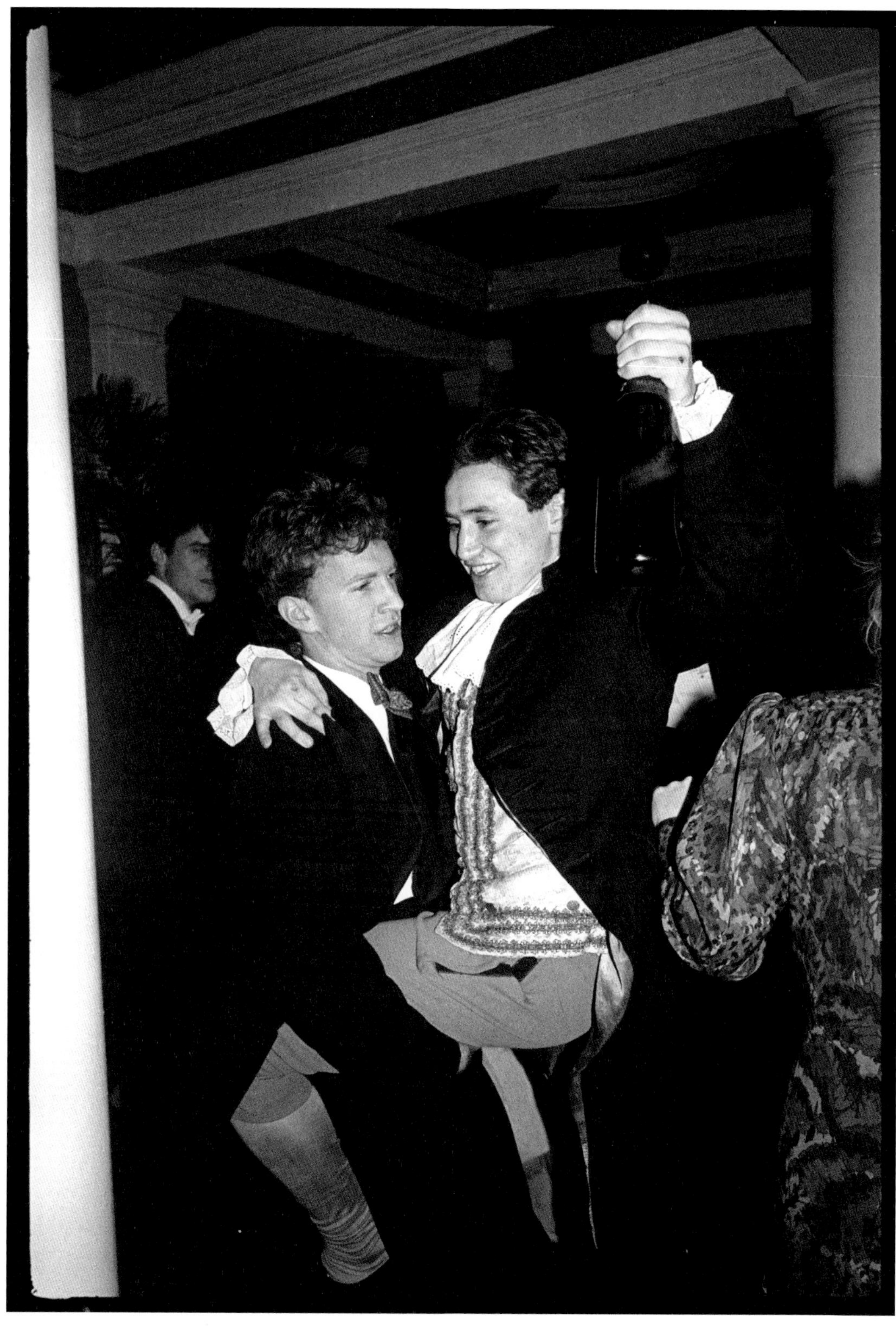

Simon Sebag Montefiore and Geoffrey Gestetner, Pitt Club Ball, 13 February 1987

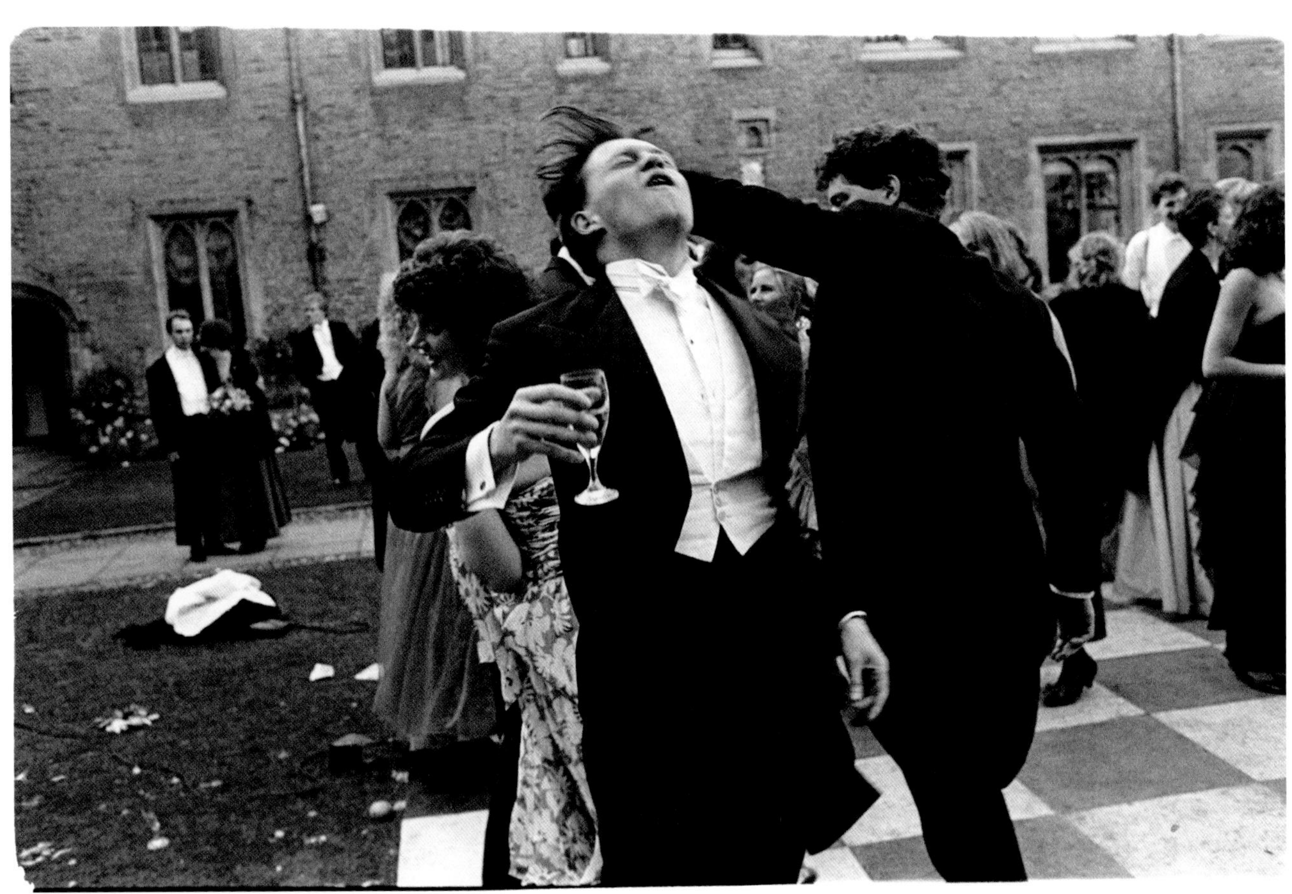

Derek Wilson dancing during the Magdalene May Ball, 17 June 1987

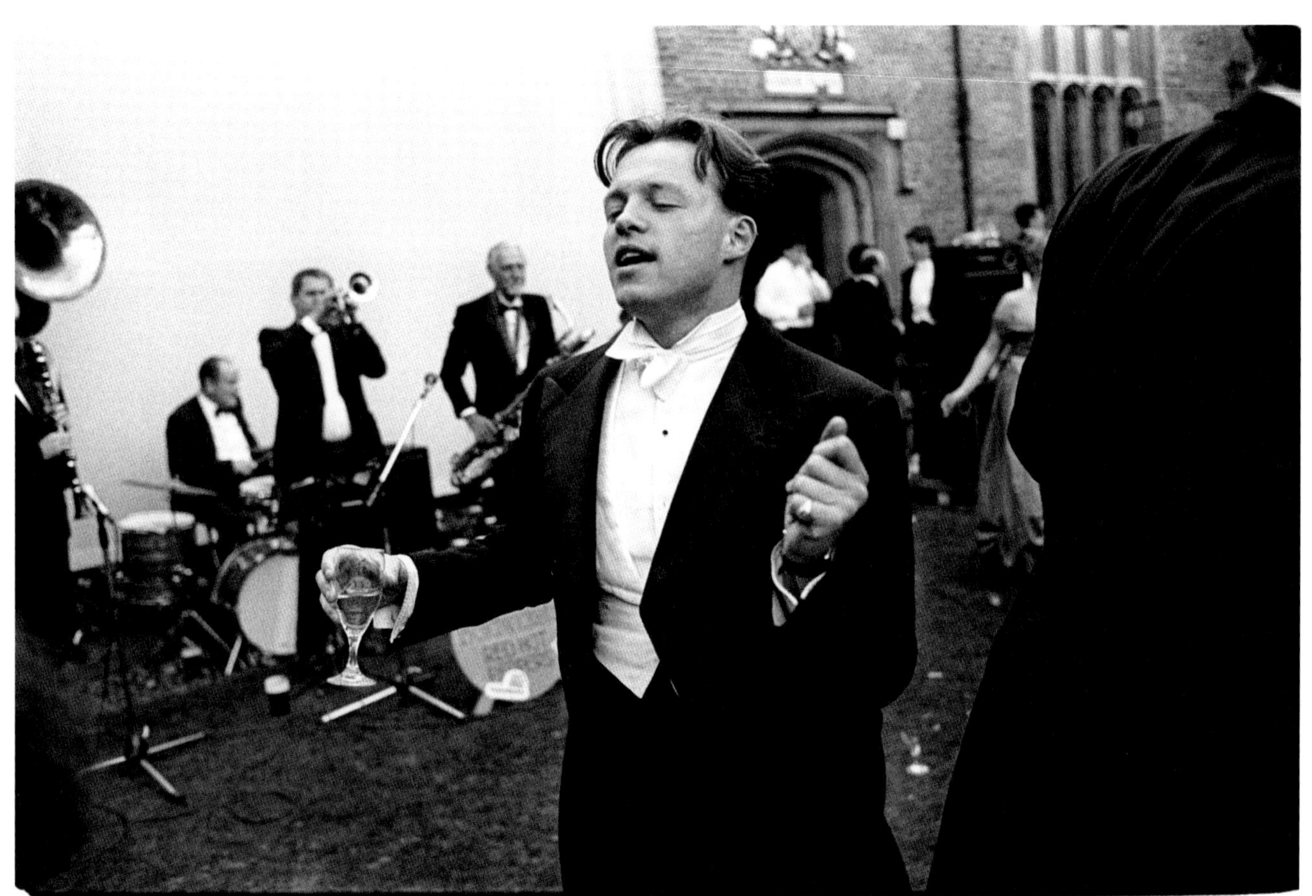

Derek Wilson dancing during the Magdalene May Ball, 17 June 1987

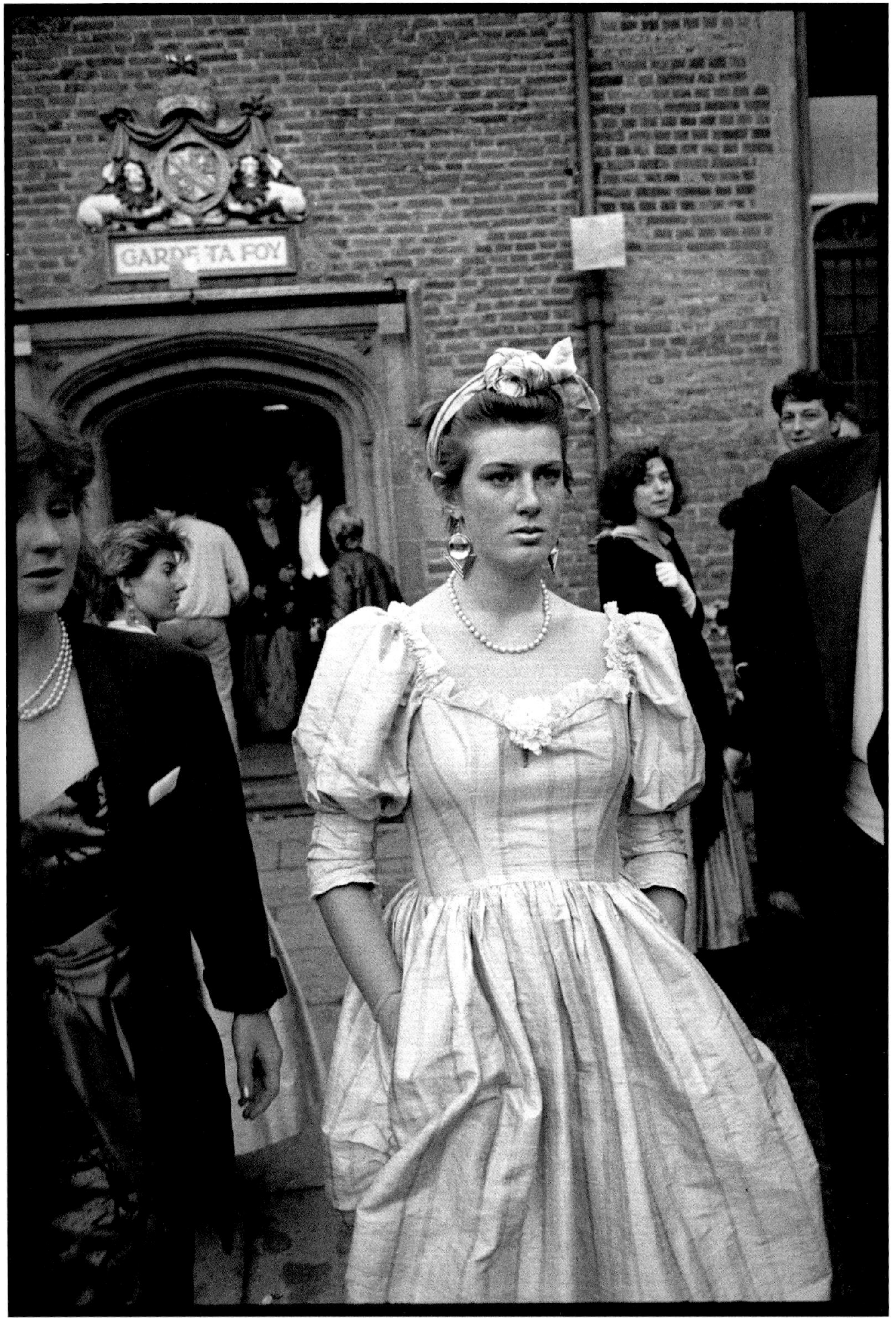

Polly Hawkes, Magdalene May Ball, 17 June 1987

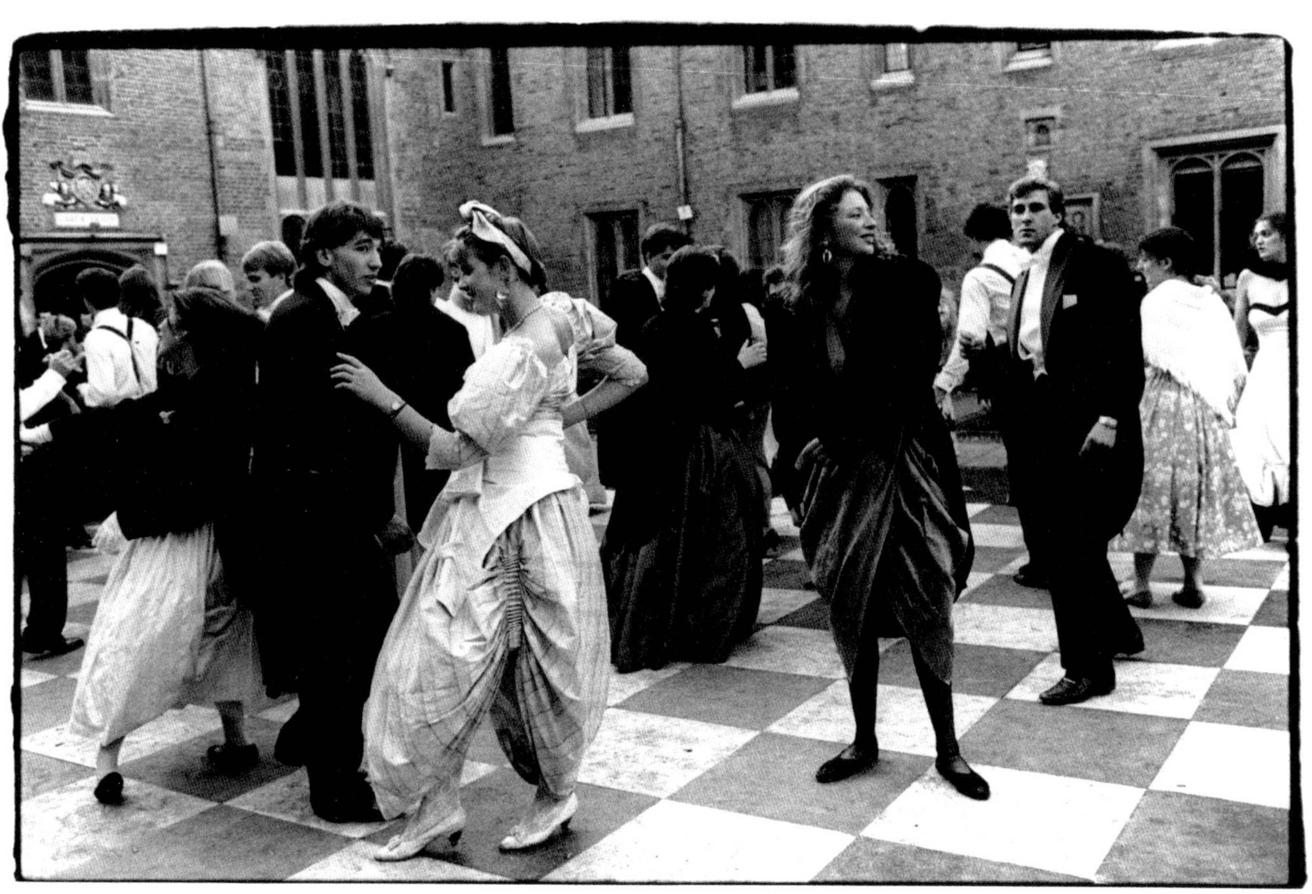

Magdalene May Ball, 17 June 1987

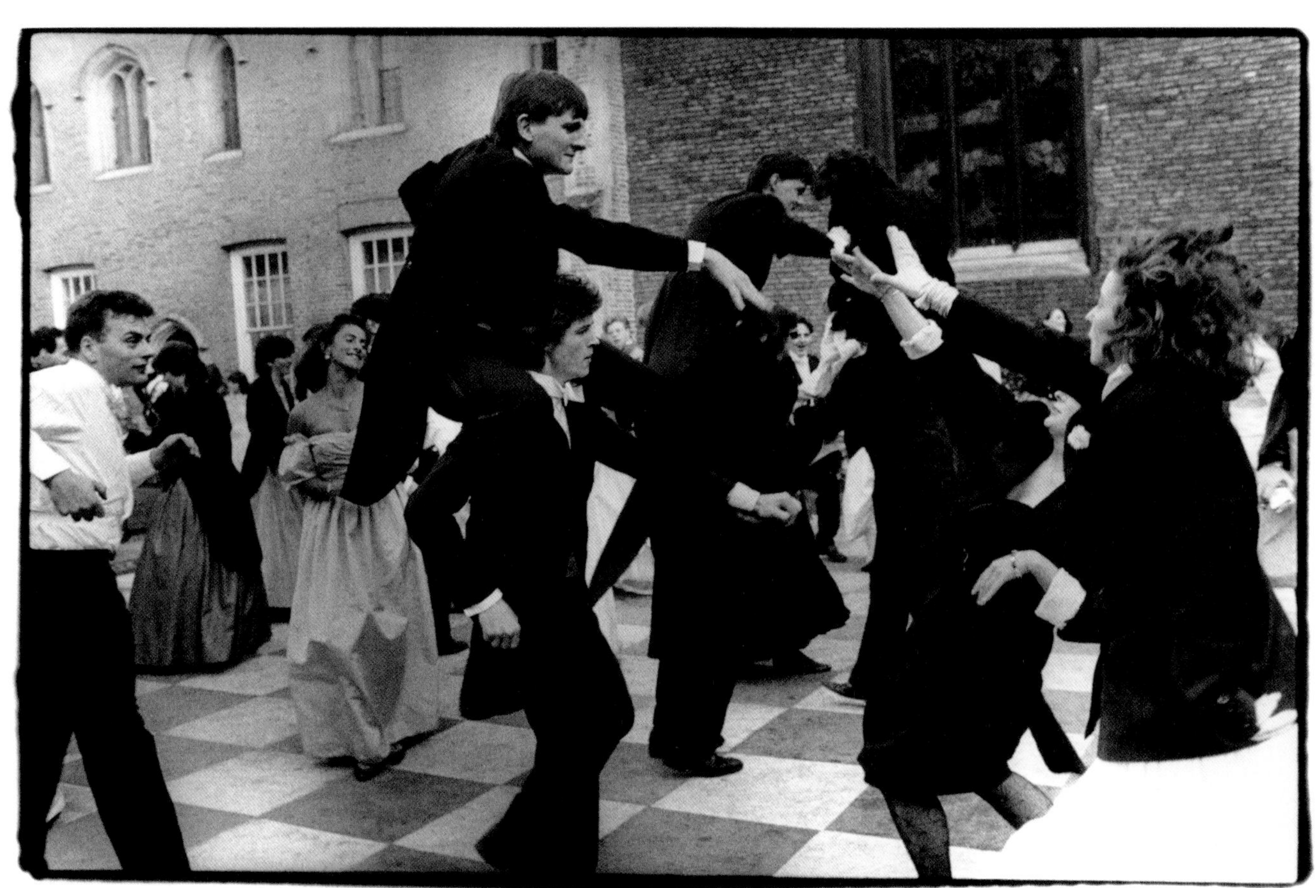

Magdalene May Ball, 17 June 1987

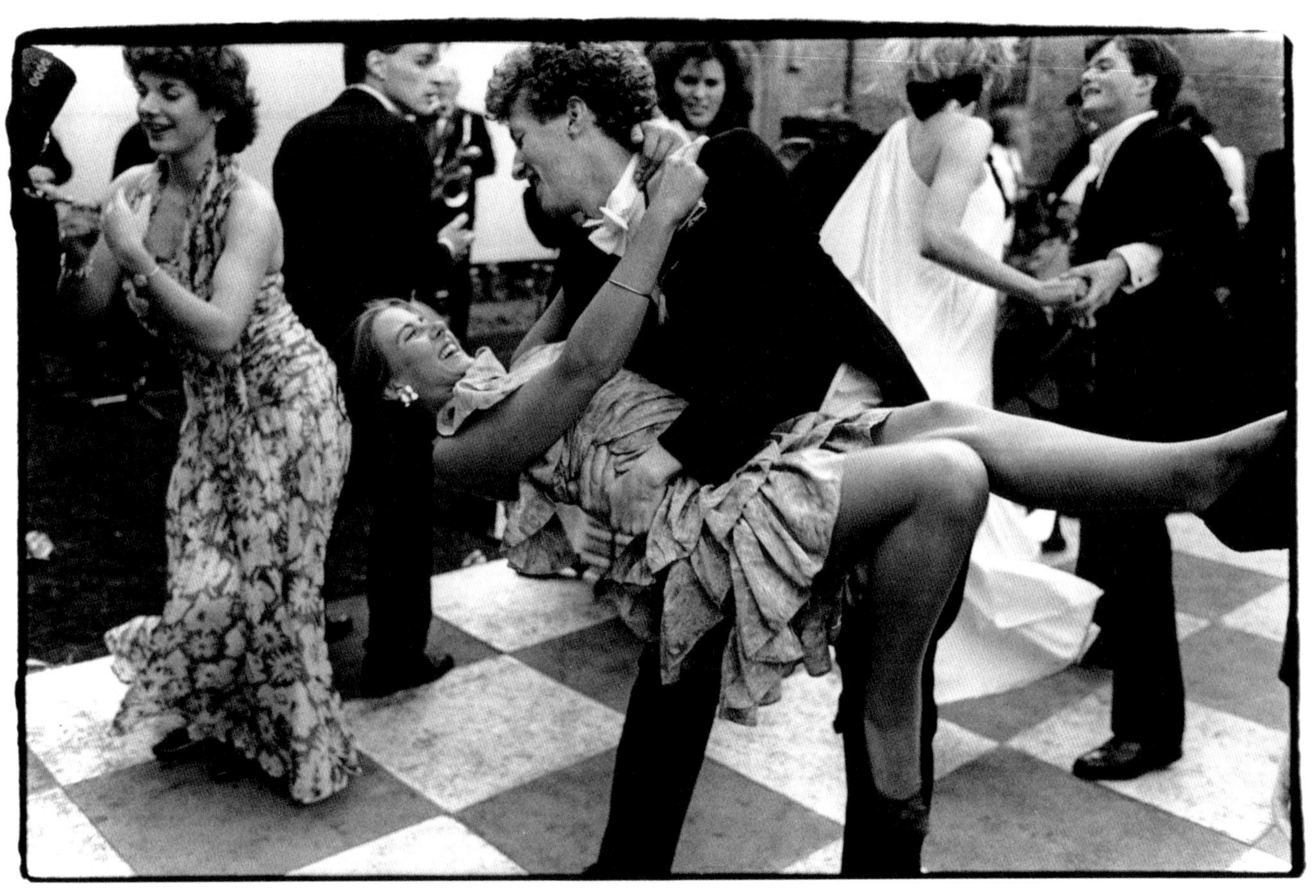

Orlando Fraser and Samantha Angus, Magdalene May Ball, 17 June 1987

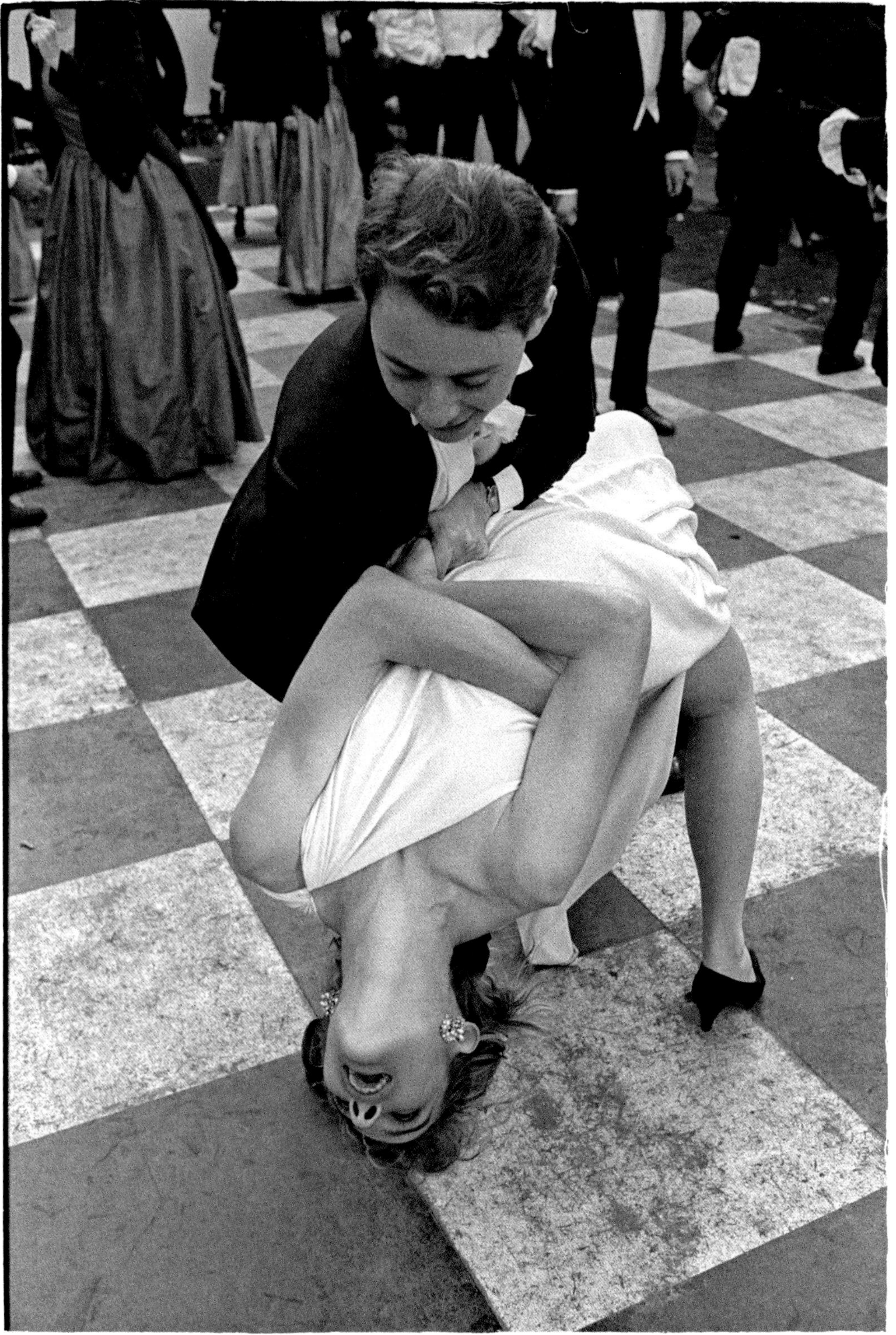

Andrew Soloman and Julie Sheehan, Magdalene May Ball, 17 June 1987

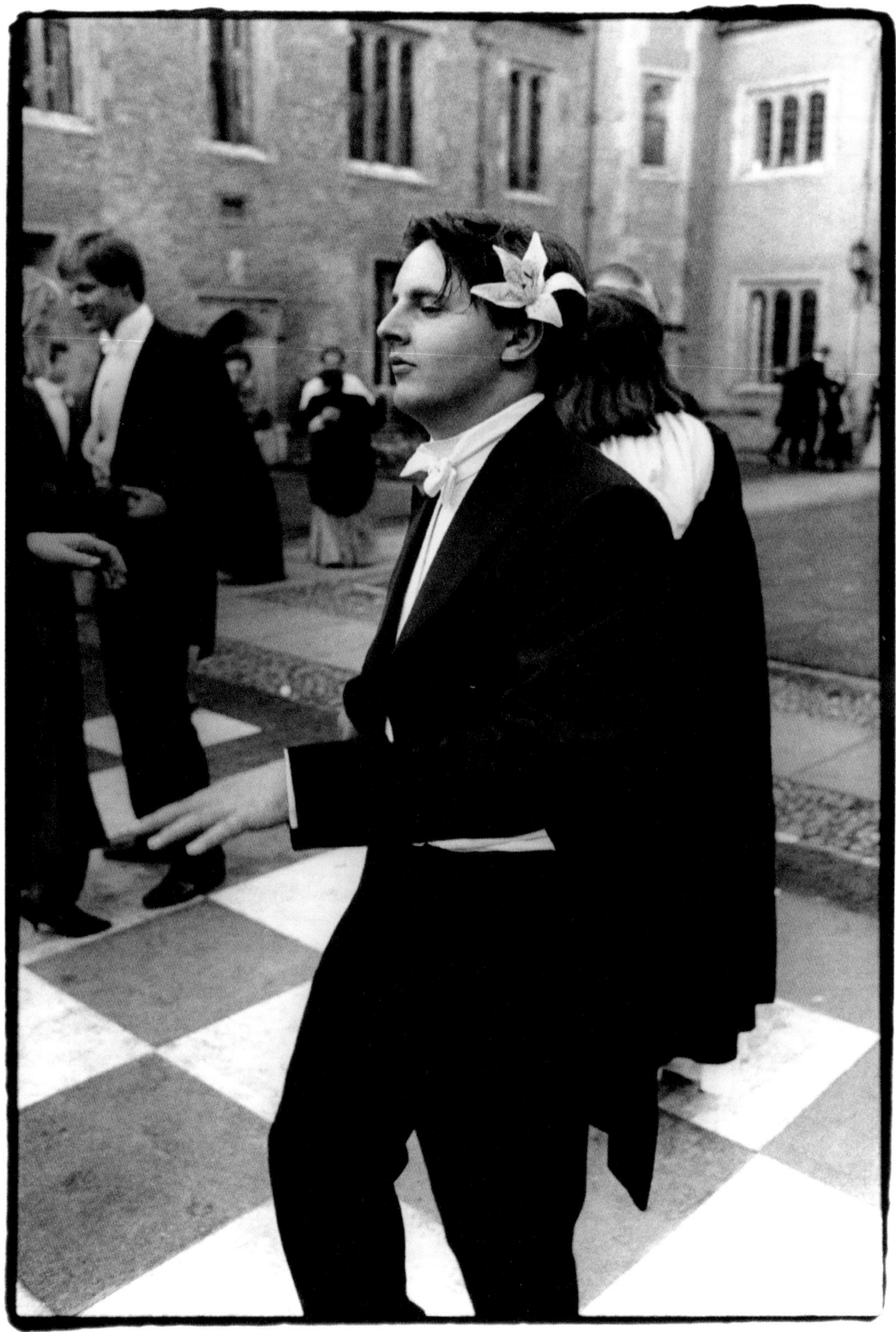

Michael Causton dancing during the Magdalene May Ball, 17 June 1987

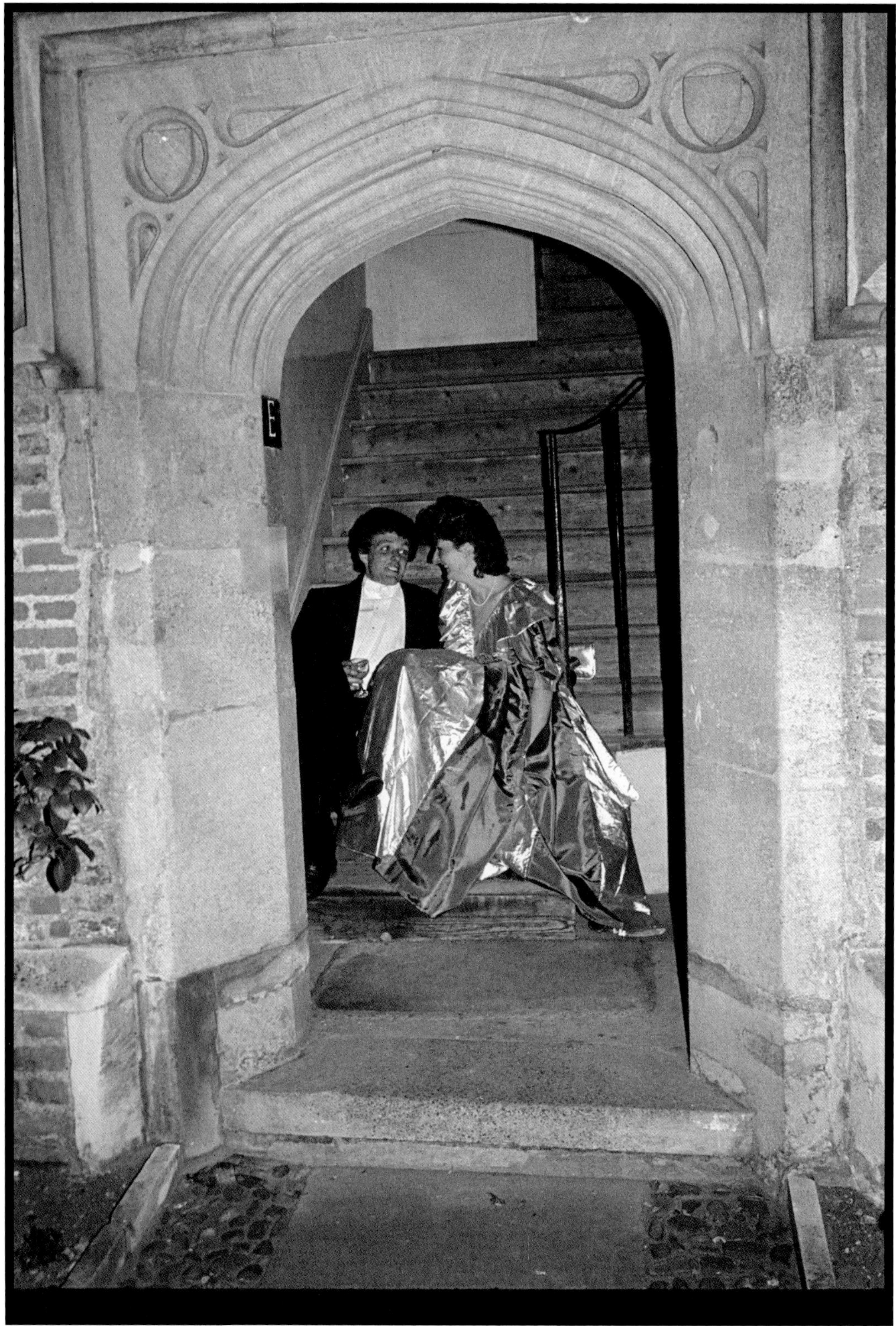

Jane Iveson and Simon Feather, Magdalene May Ball, 15 June 1983

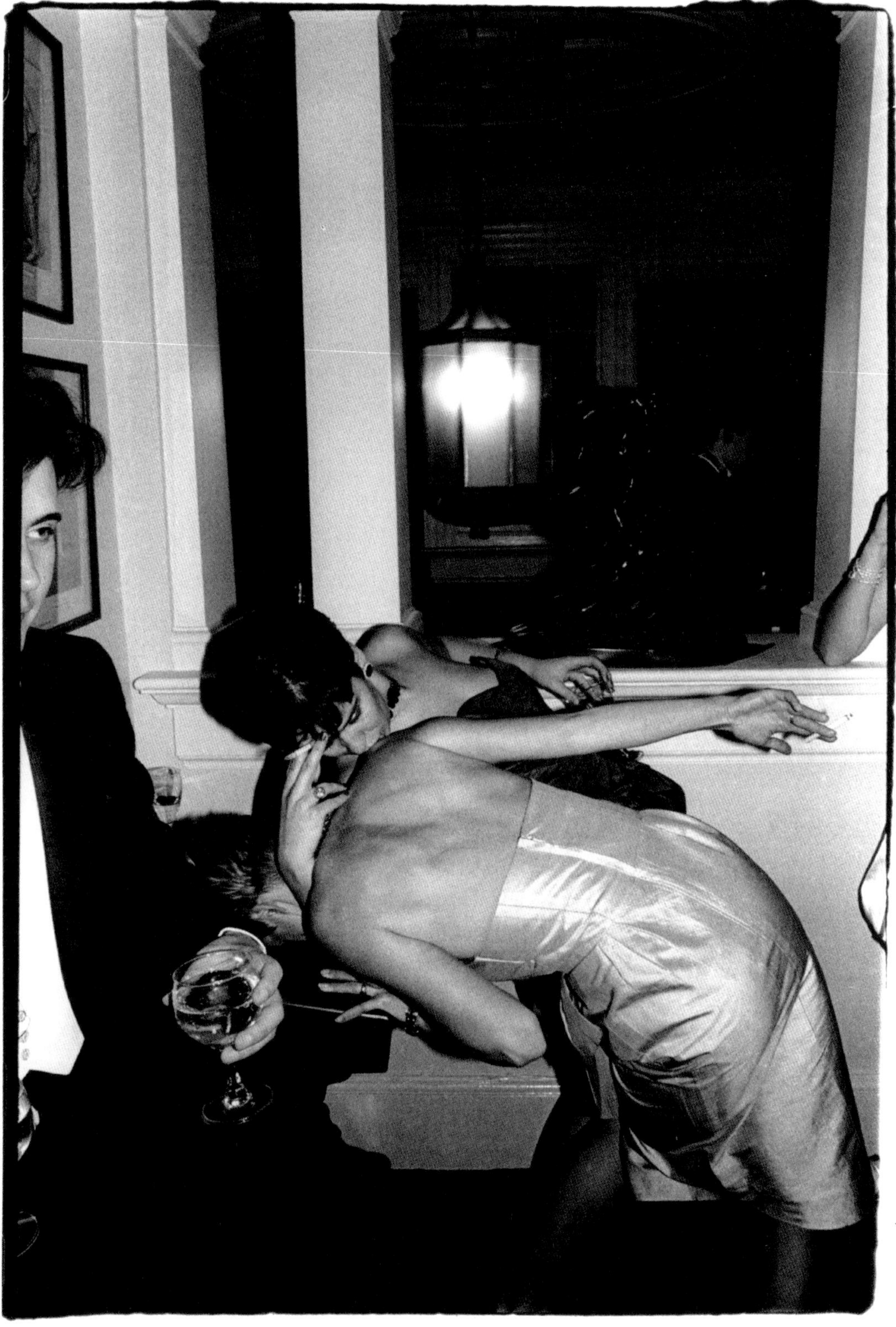

Pitt Club Ball, February 1988

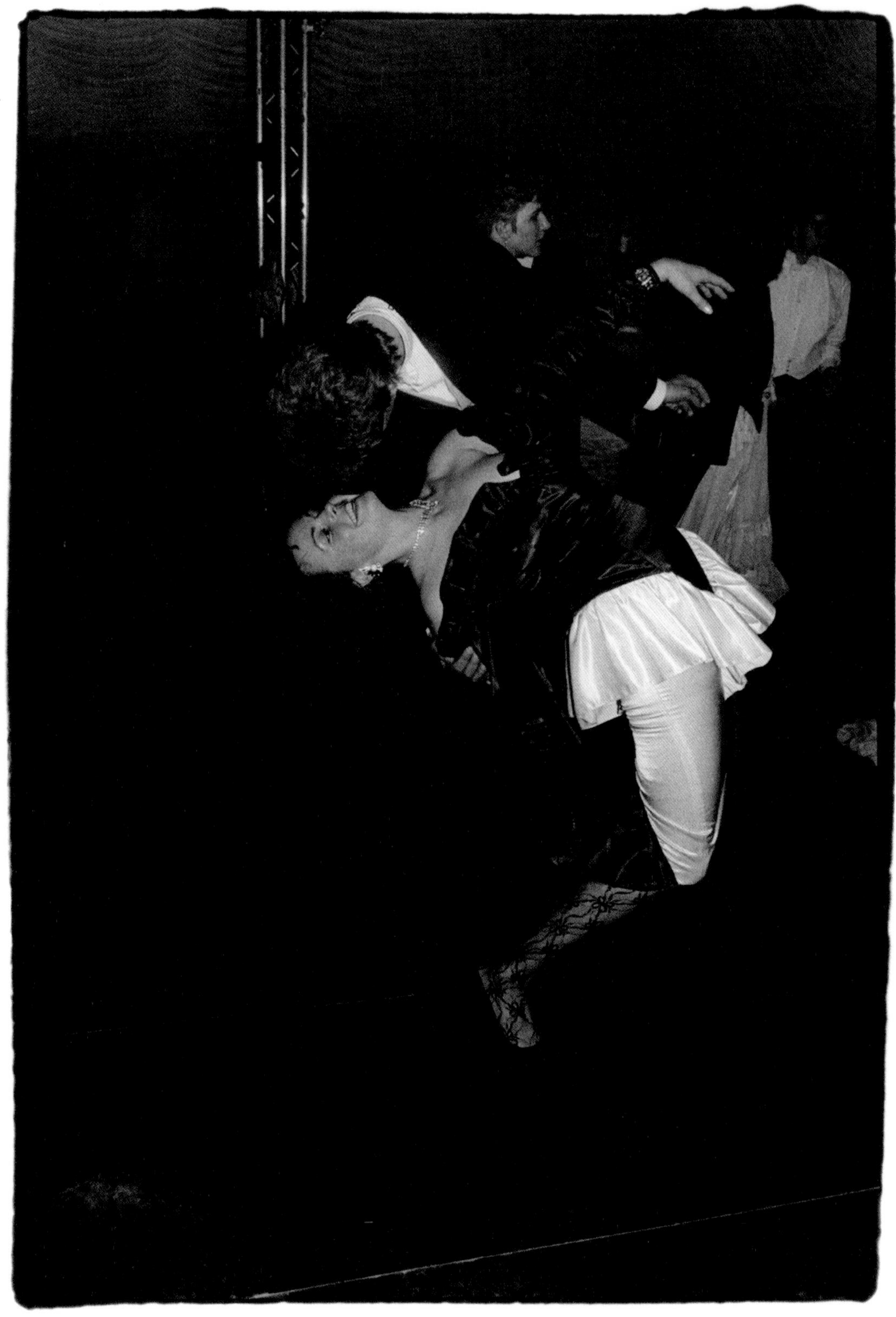

Rosanna Palmer dancing with Giles Whitworth during the Magdalene May Ball, 17 June 1987

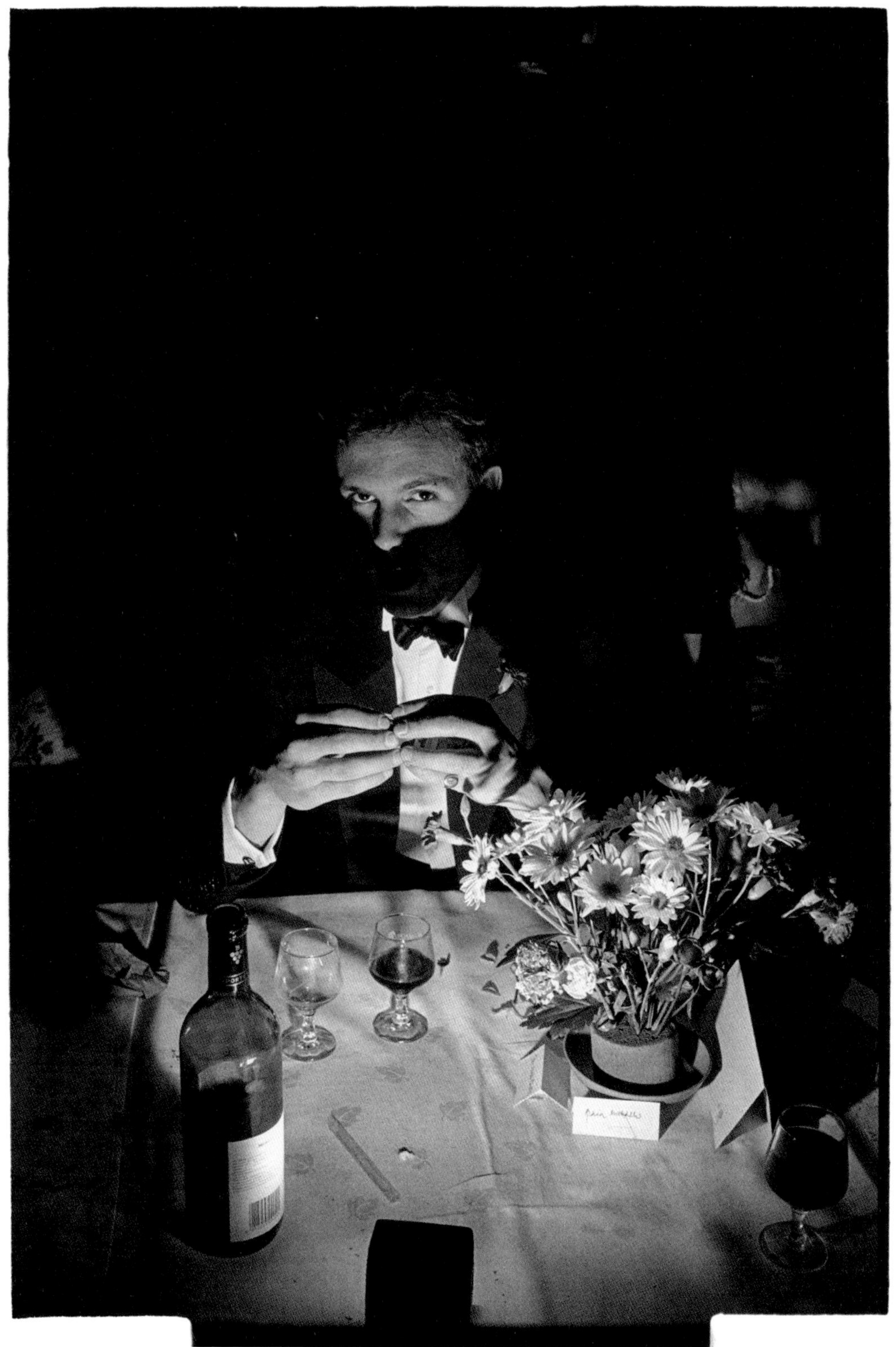

Toby Mansel-Pleydell, Cambridge Hunt Club Ball, Chilford Barns, Linton, 4 March 1988

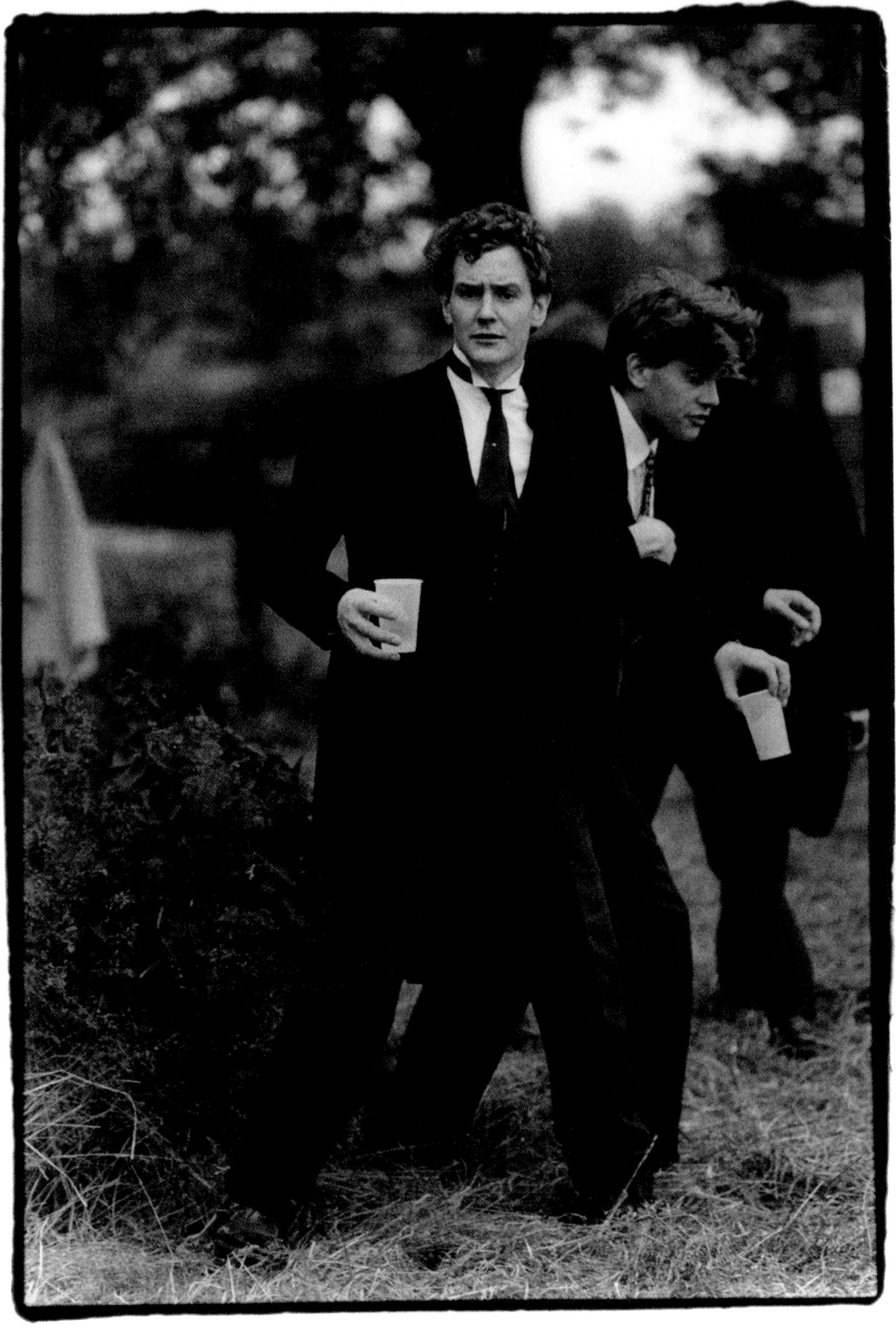

Dominic Armstrong and David St George, Wylie drinks party, Grantchester Meadows, 11 June 1988

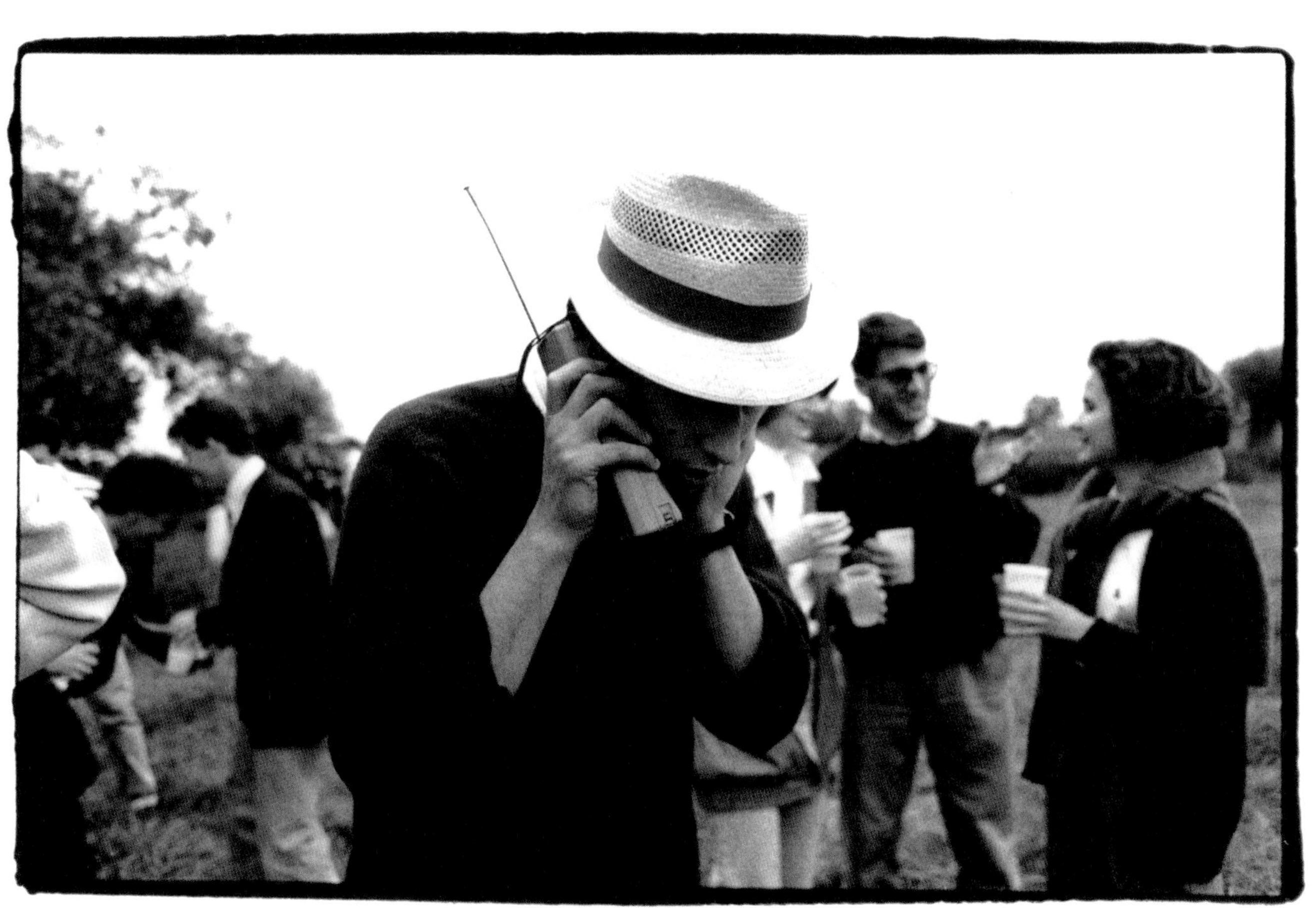

Carl Baum, Wylie drinks party, Granchester Meadows, 11 June 1988

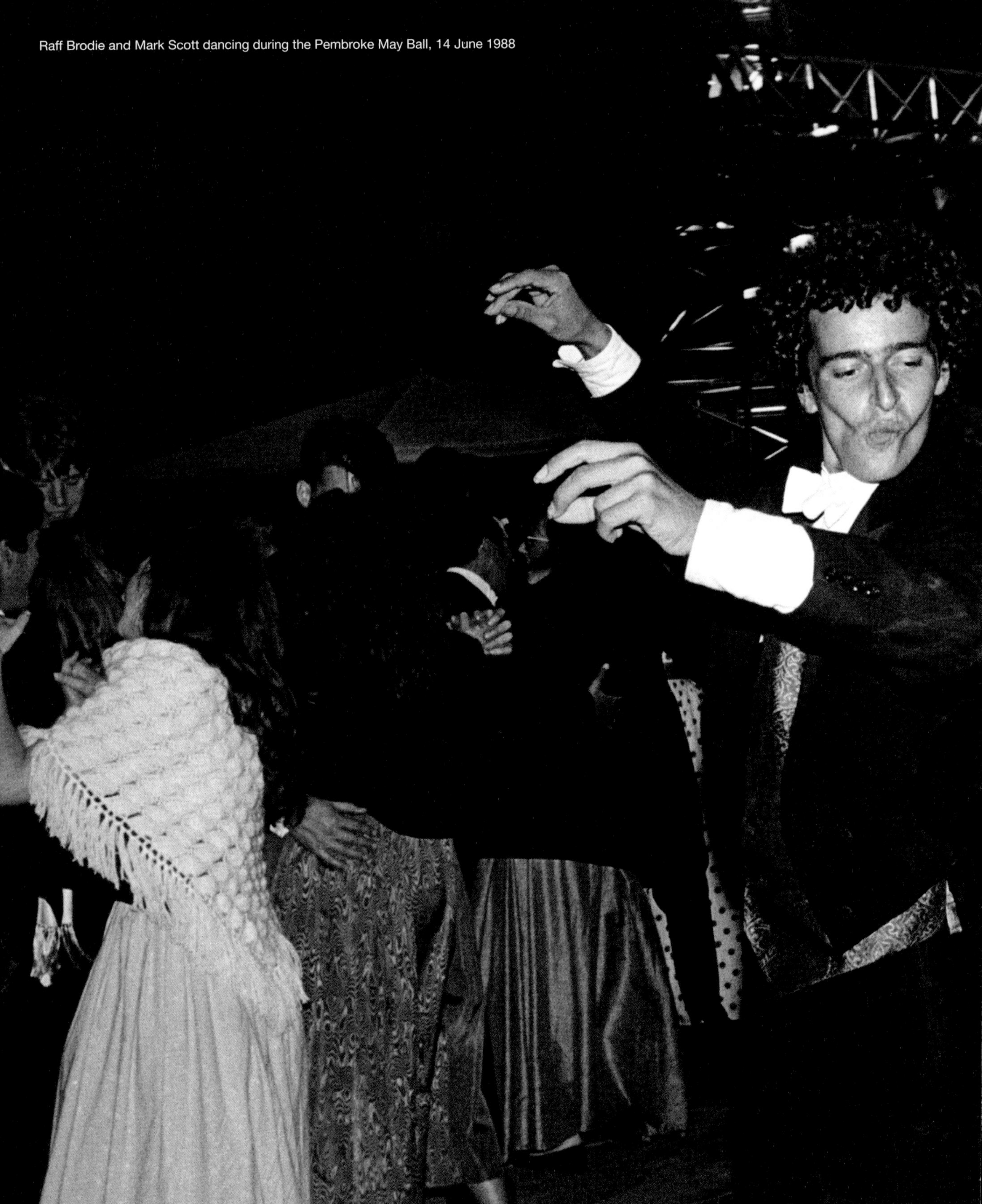

Raff Brodie and Mark Scott dancing during the Pembroke May Ball, 14 June 1988

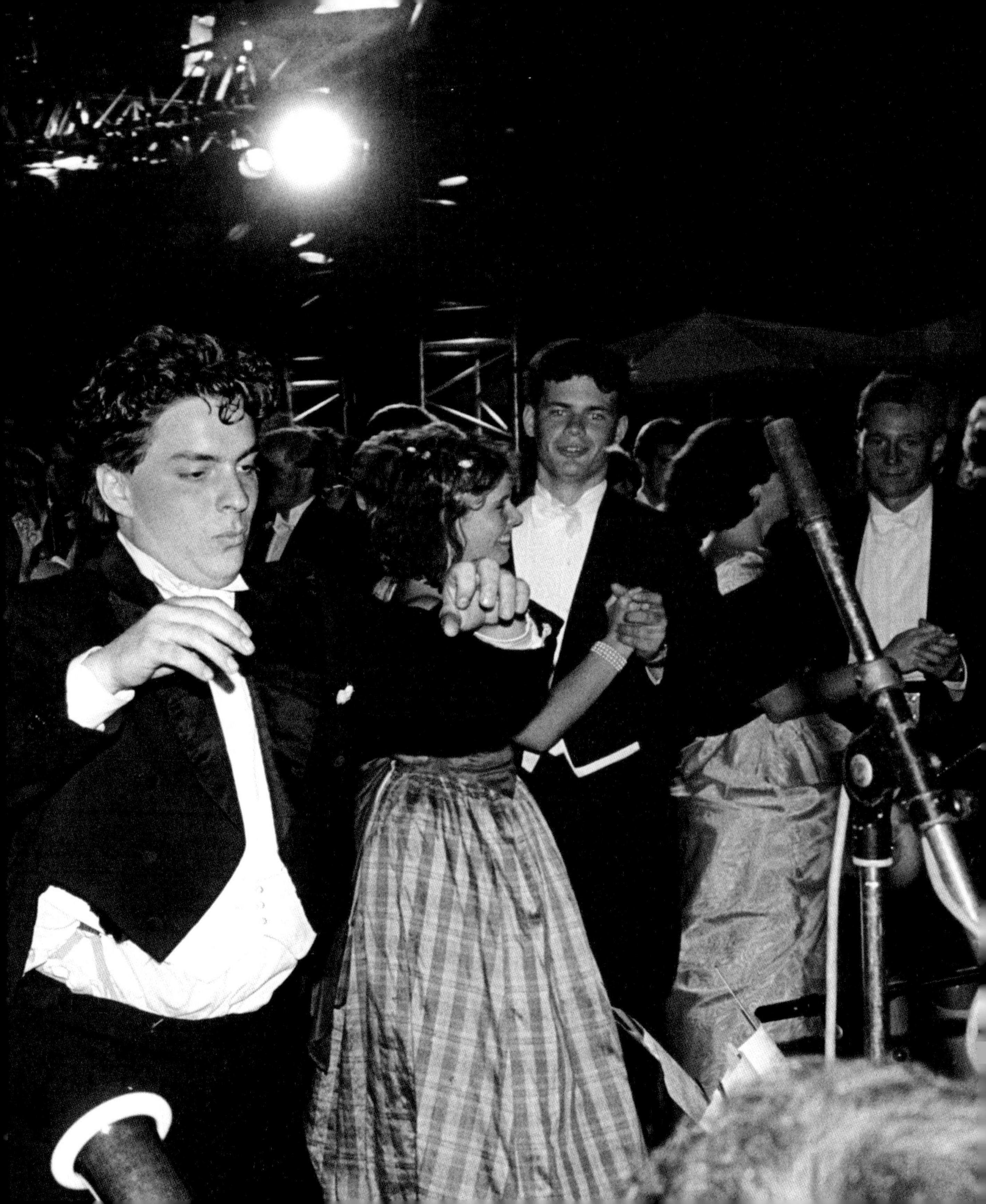

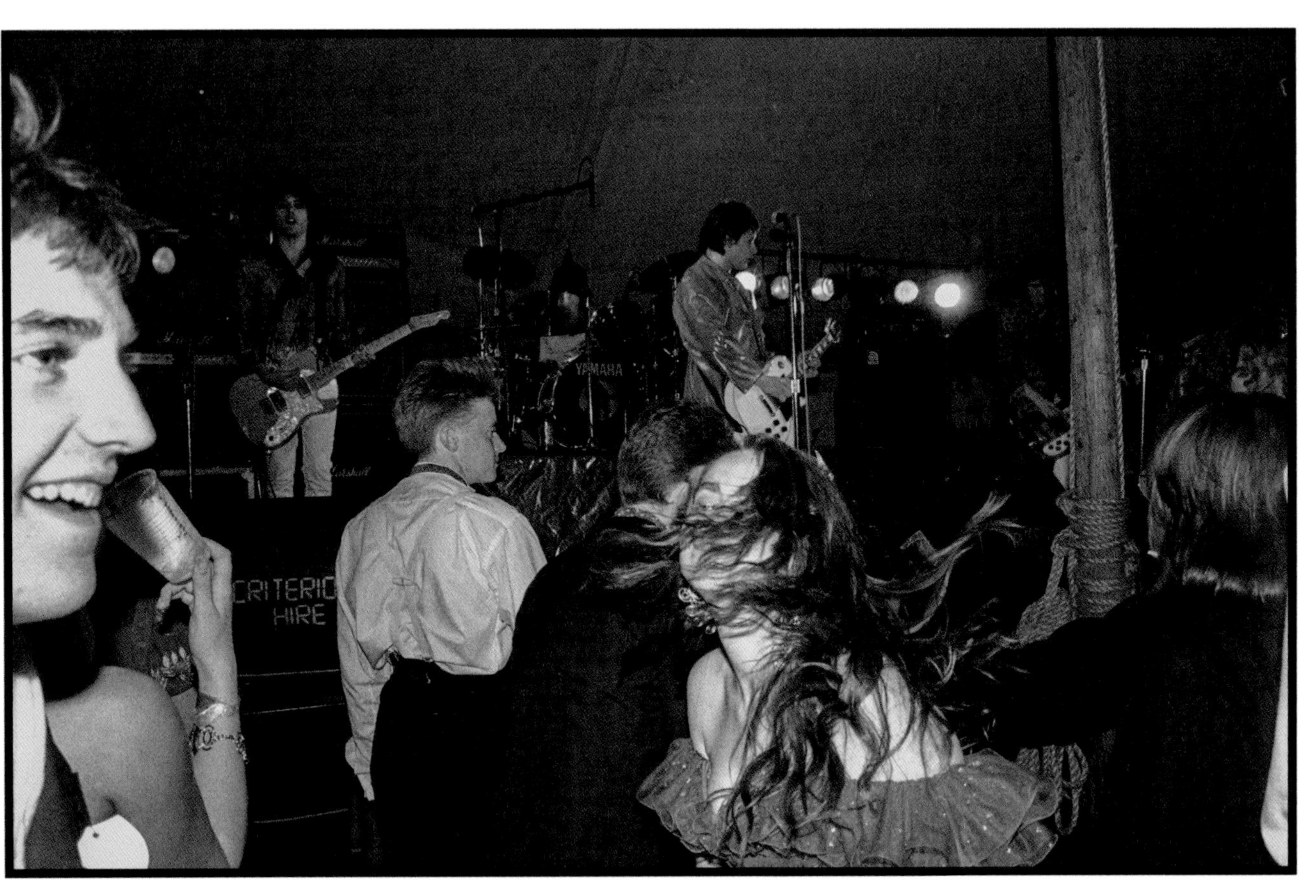

Manic Street Preachers on stage at the Downing May Ball, 17 June 1991

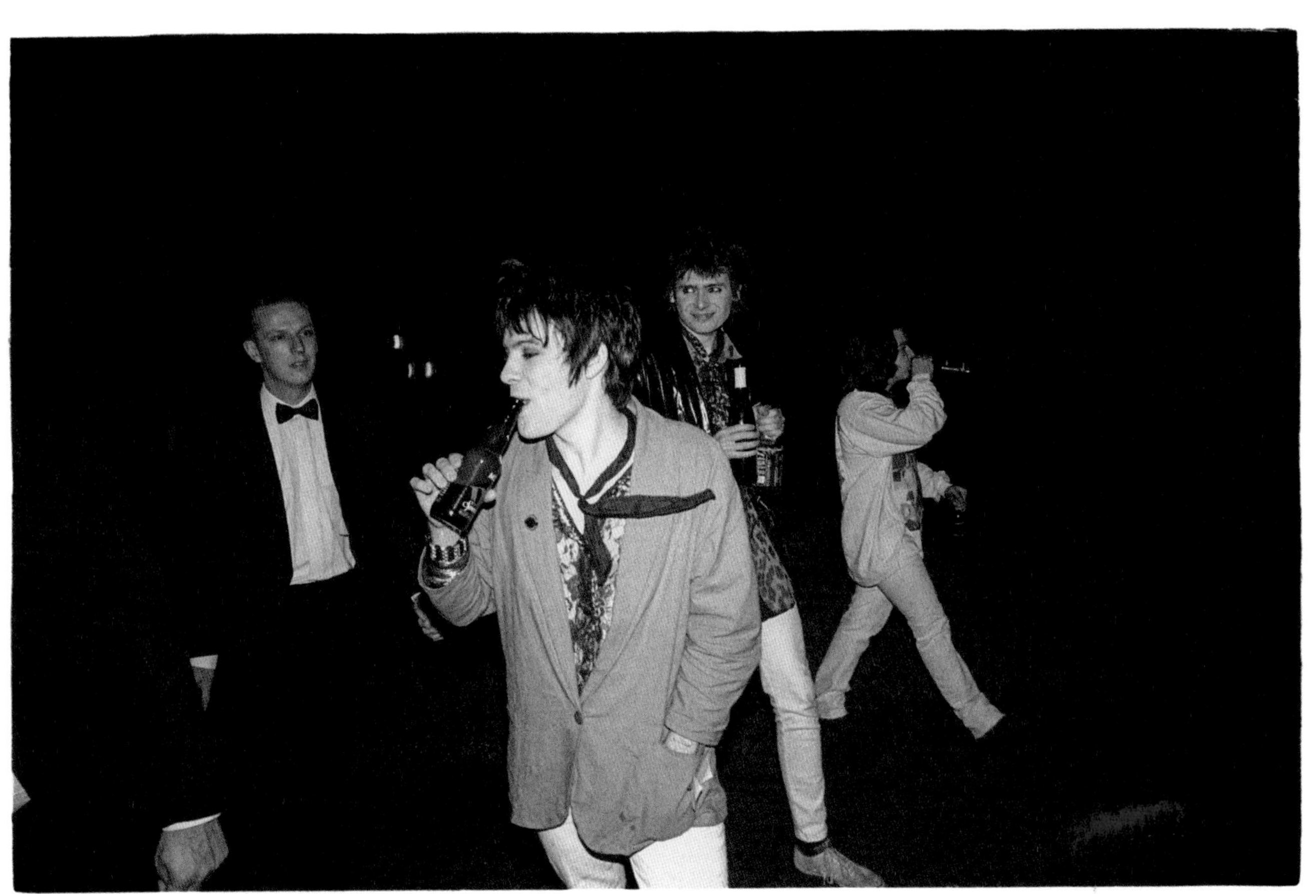

Richey Edwards of Manic Street Preachers, Downing May Ball, 17 June 1991

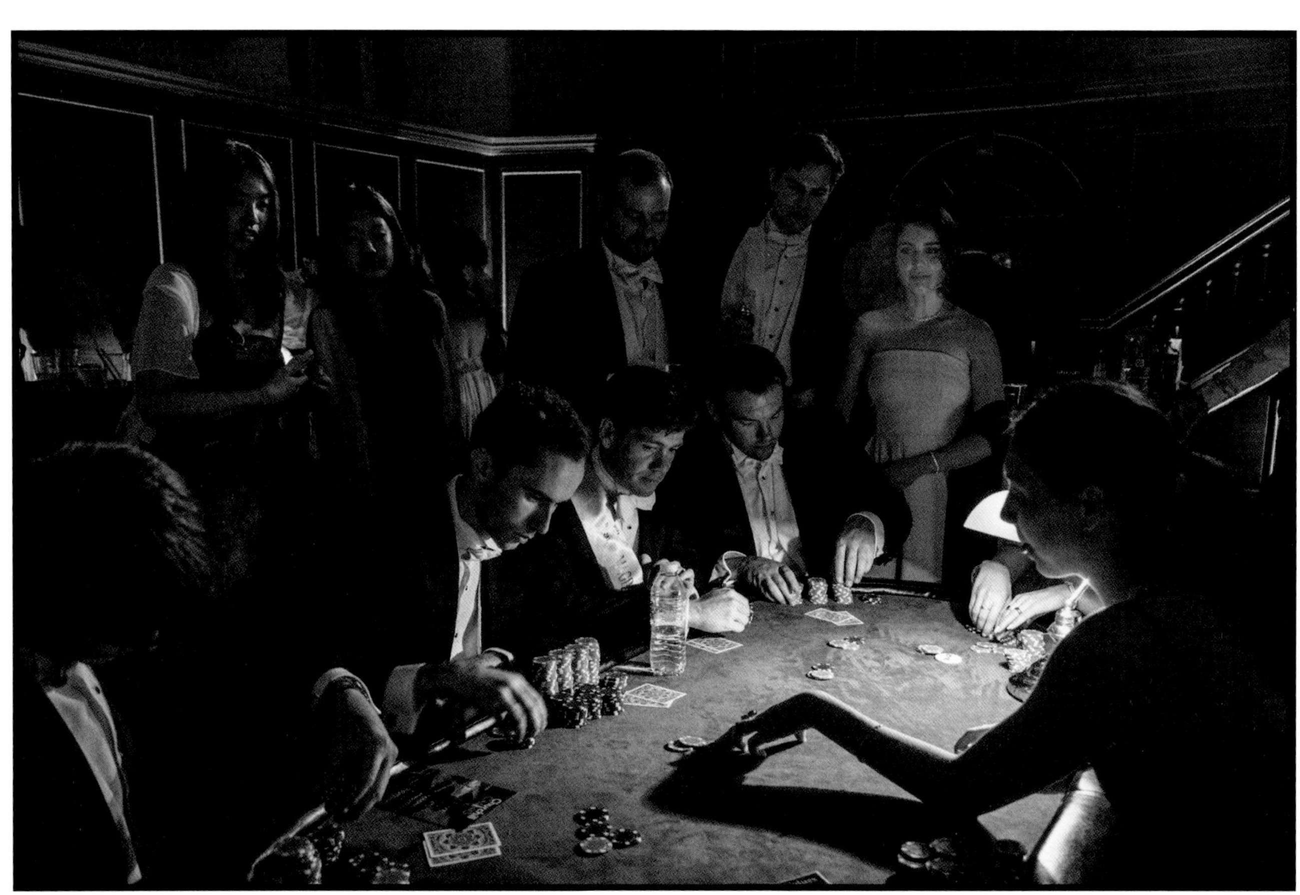

Magdalene May Ball, 25 June 2025

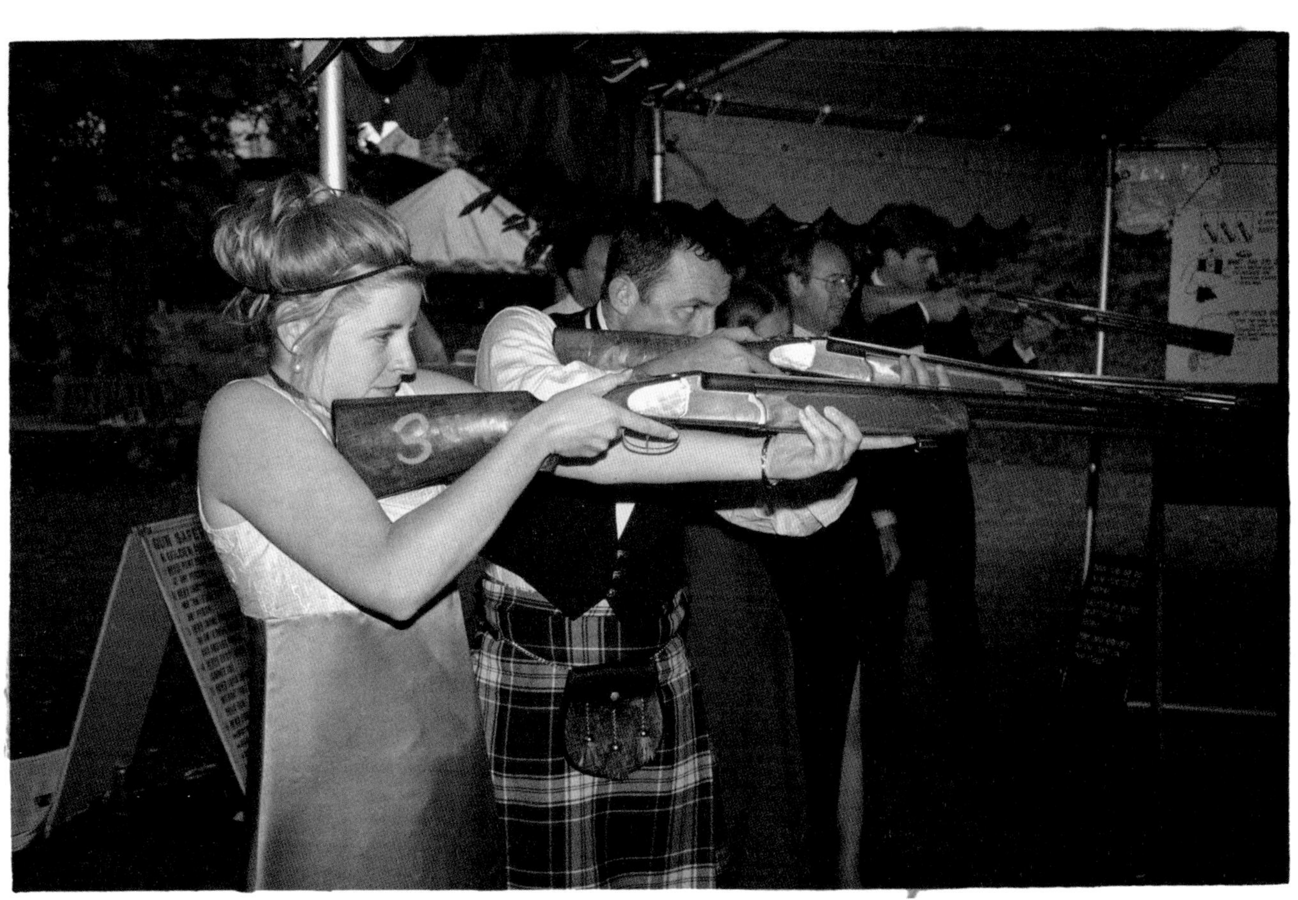

Judith Murray and Angus Main, Magdalene May Ball, 18 June 1997

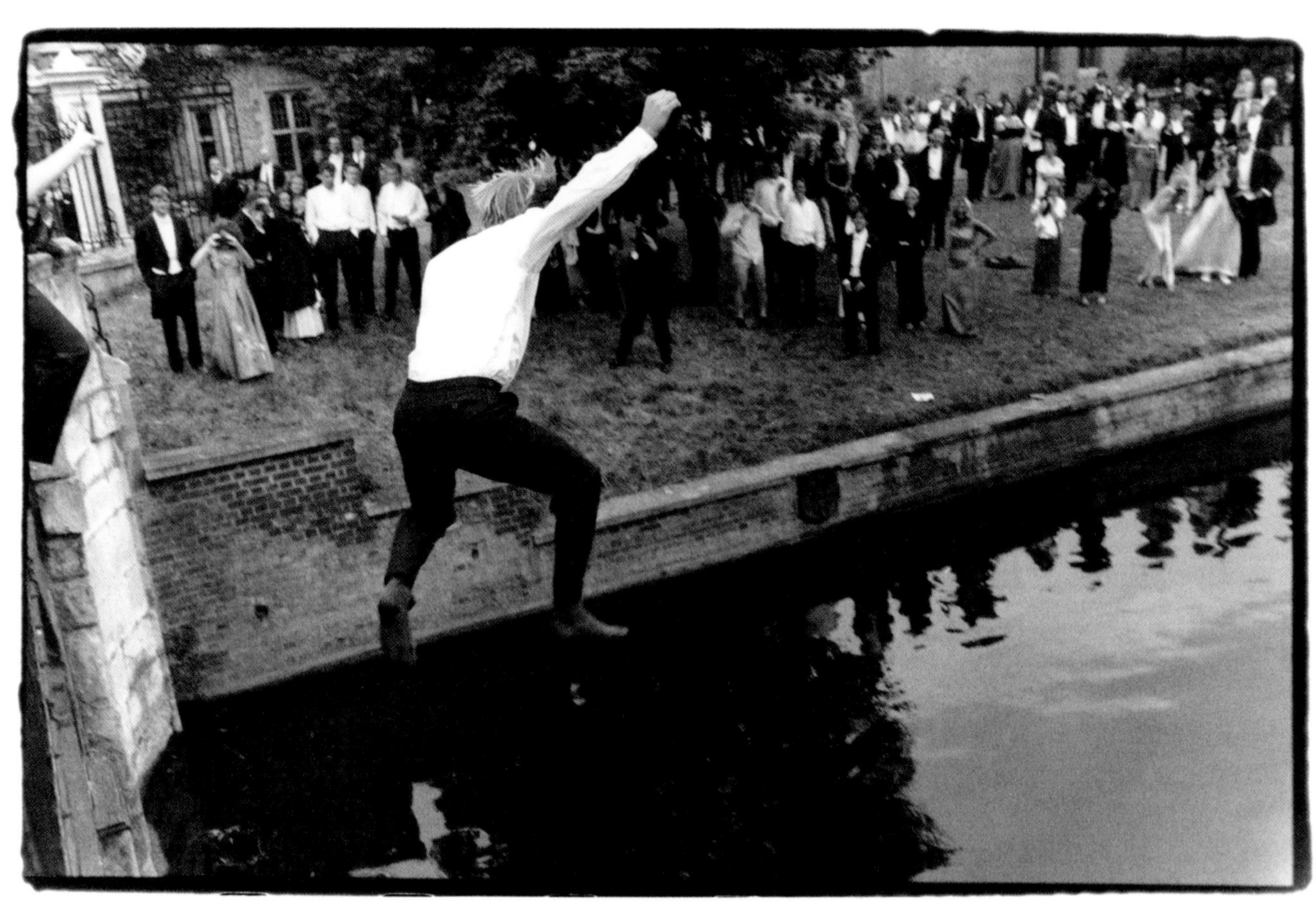

Magdalene May Ball, 18 June 1997

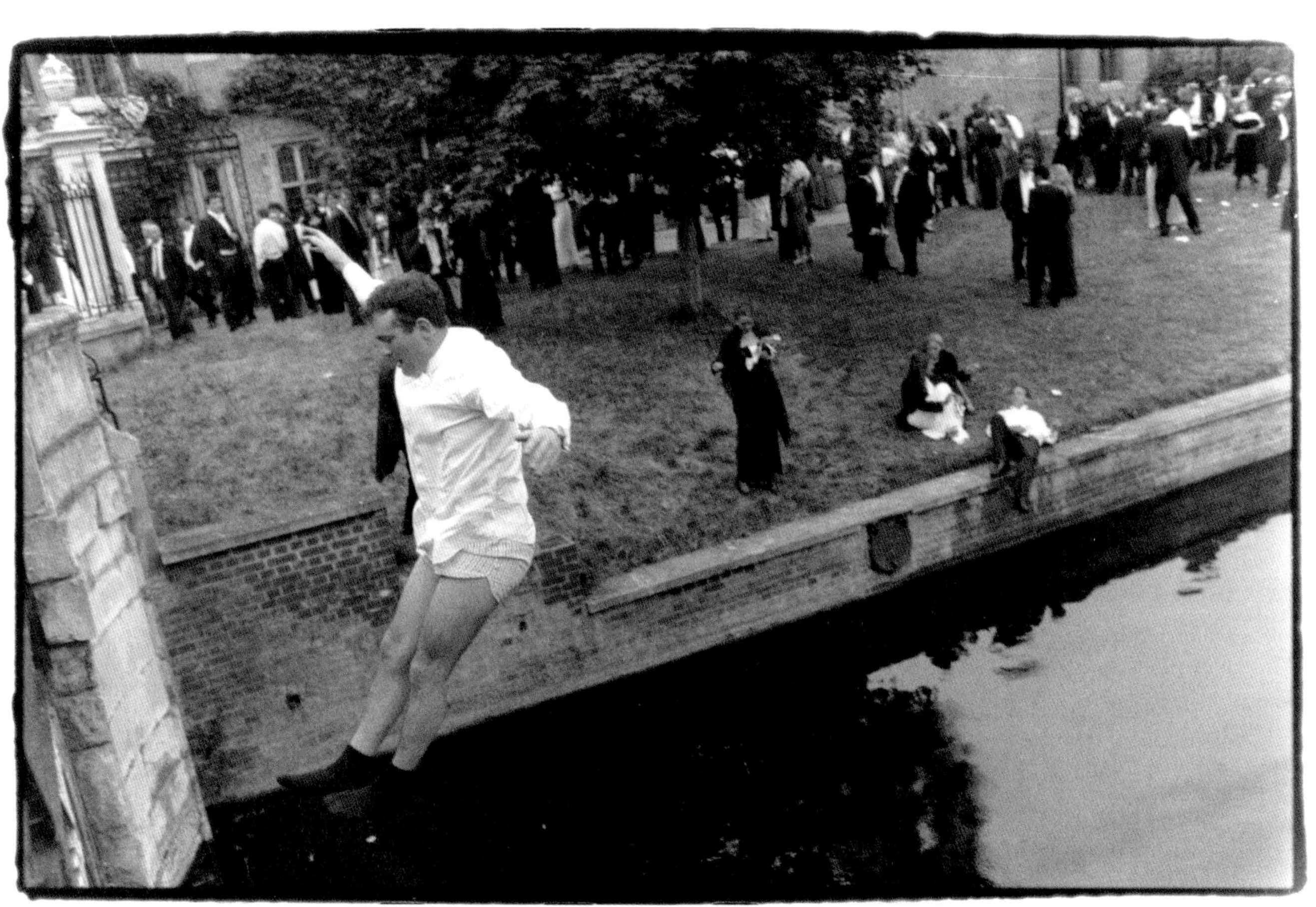

Magdalene May Ball, 18 June 1997

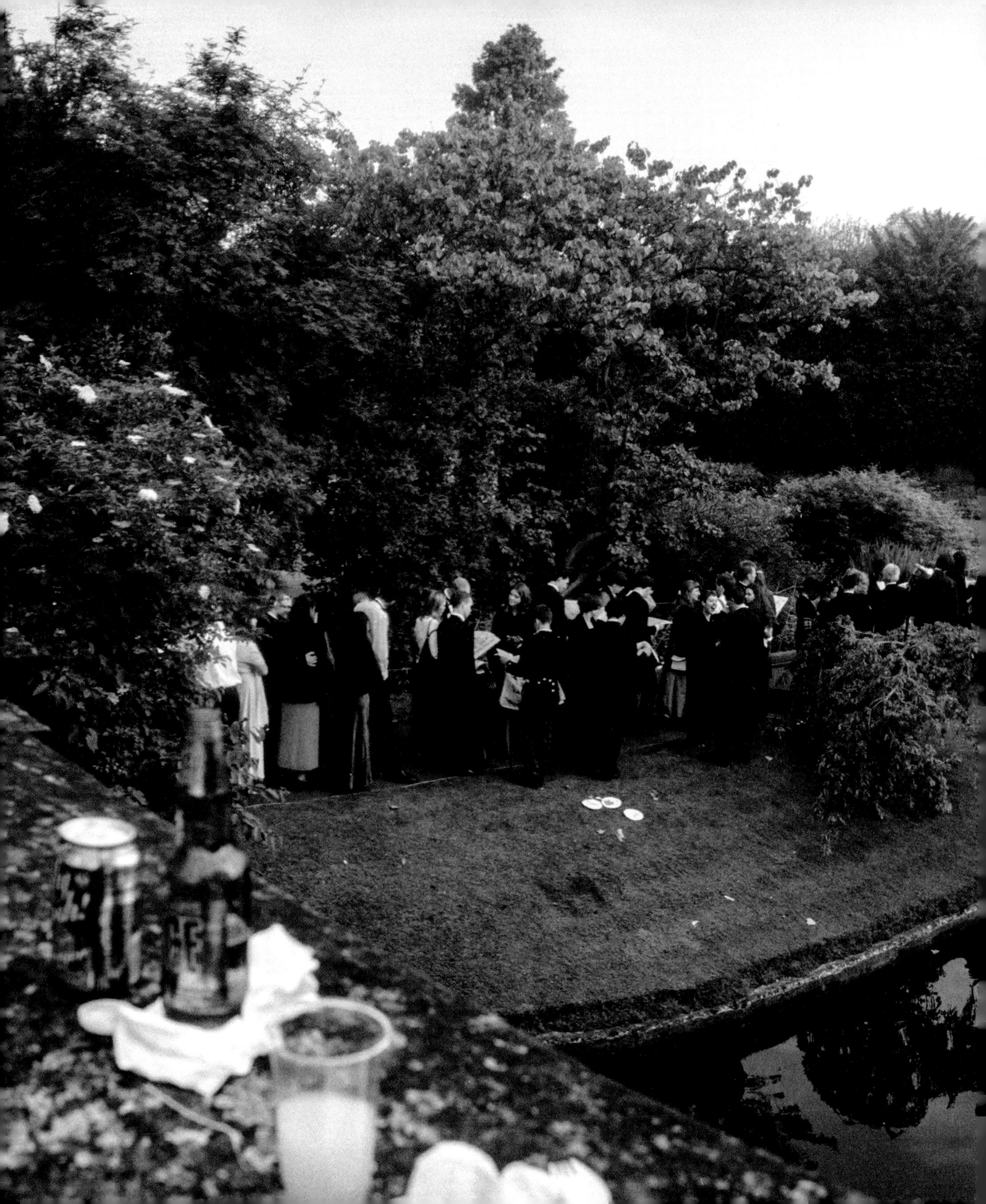

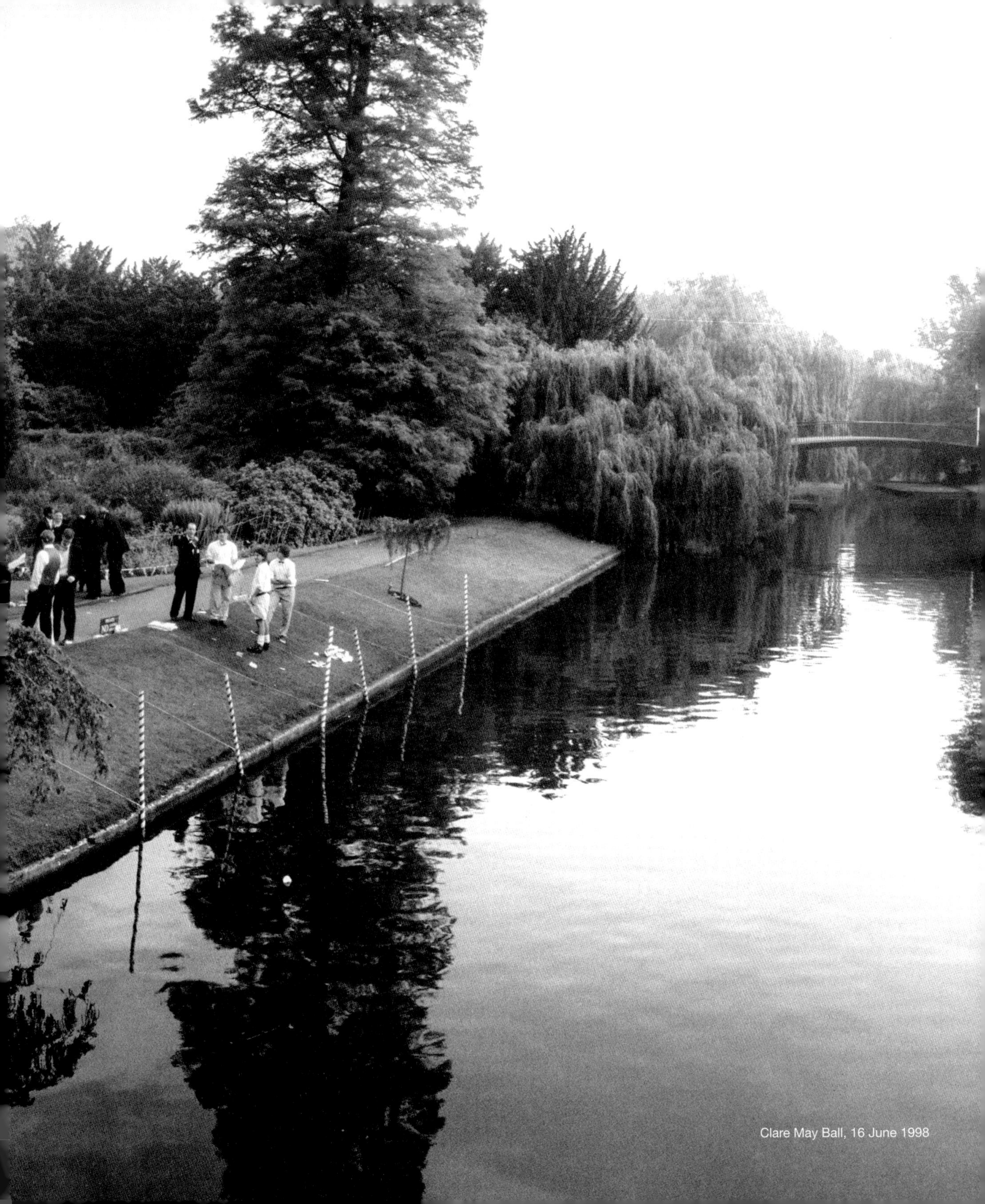

Clare May Ball, 16 June 1998

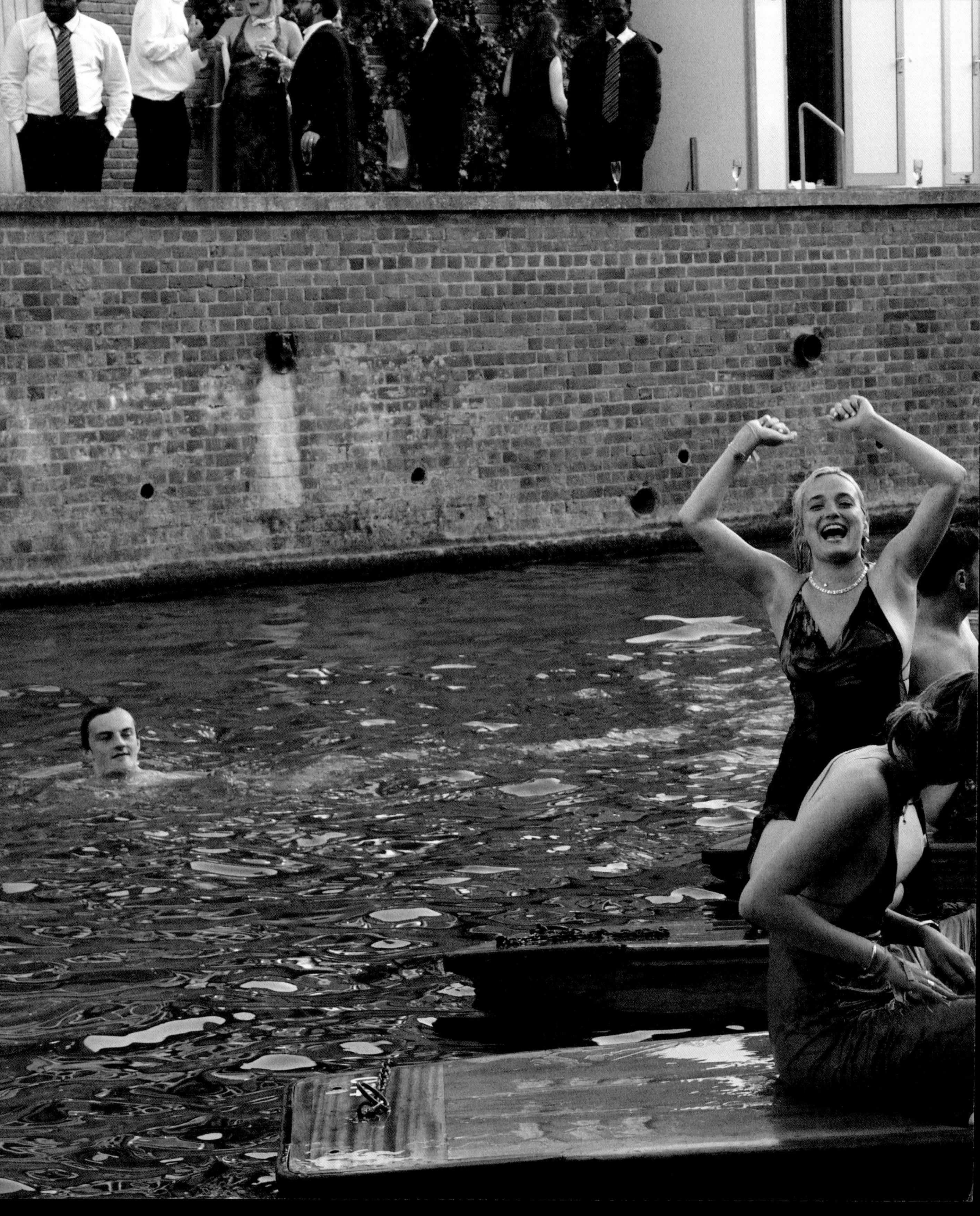

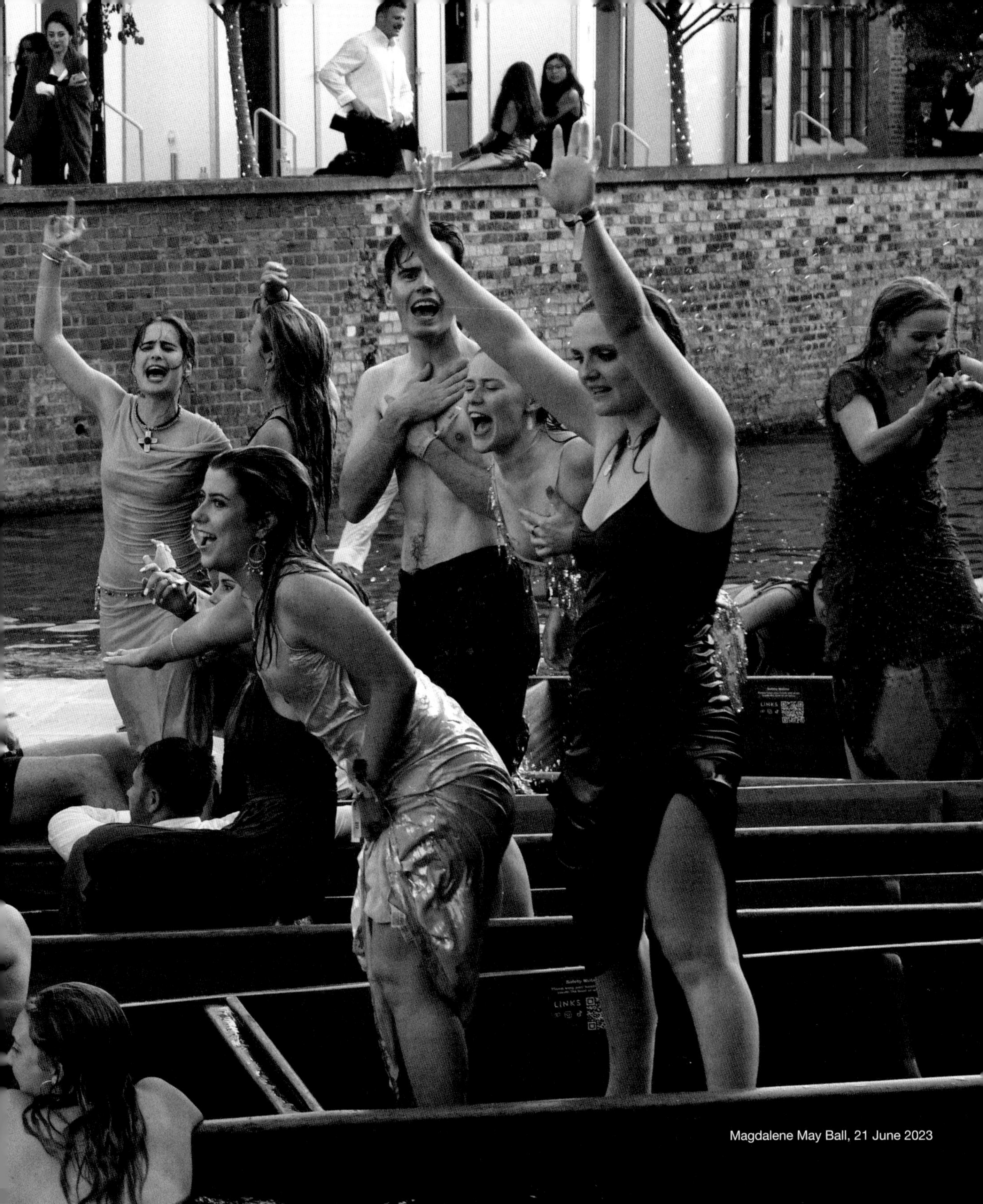

Magdalene May Ball, 21 June 2023

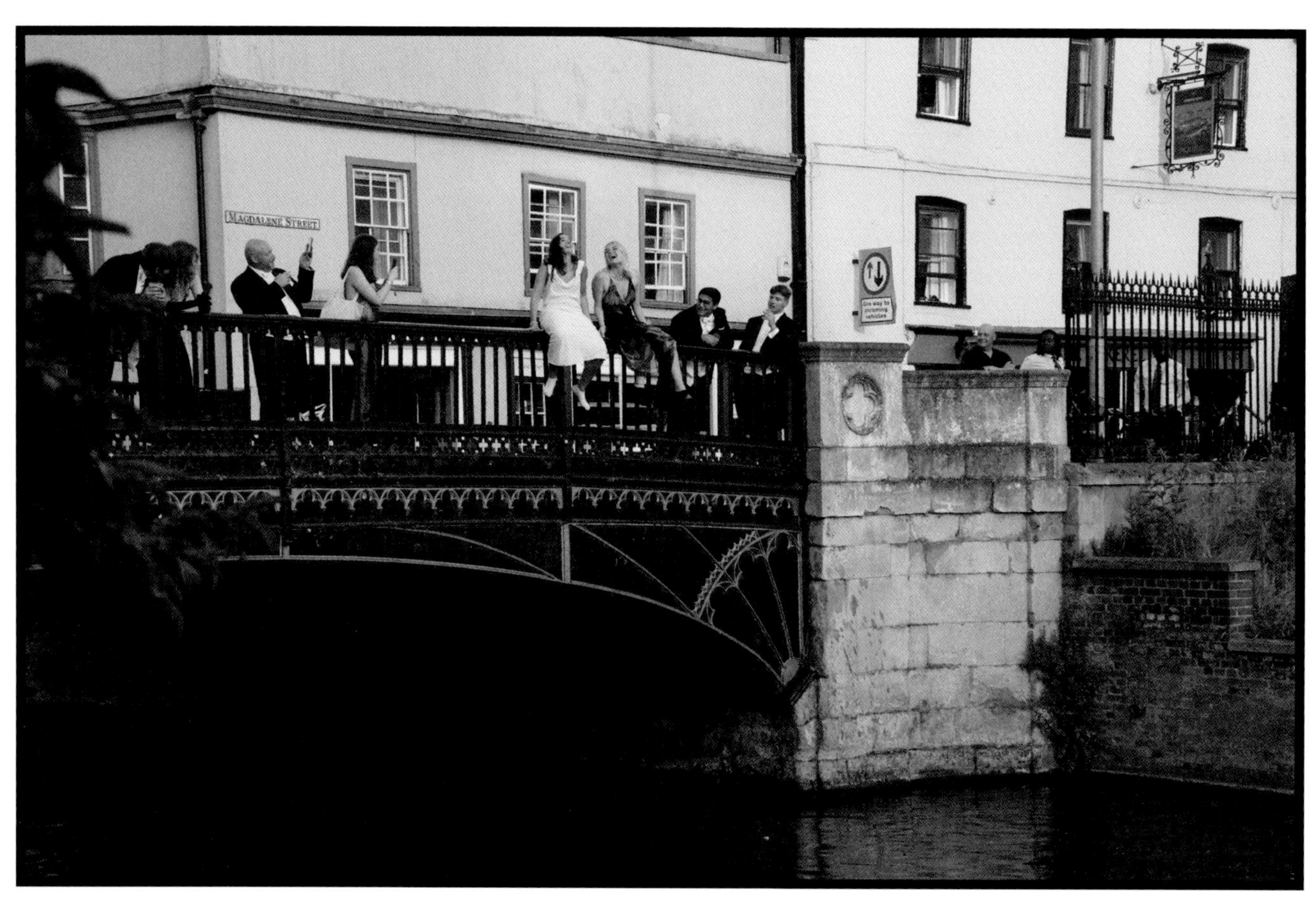

Magdalene May Ball, 21 June 2023

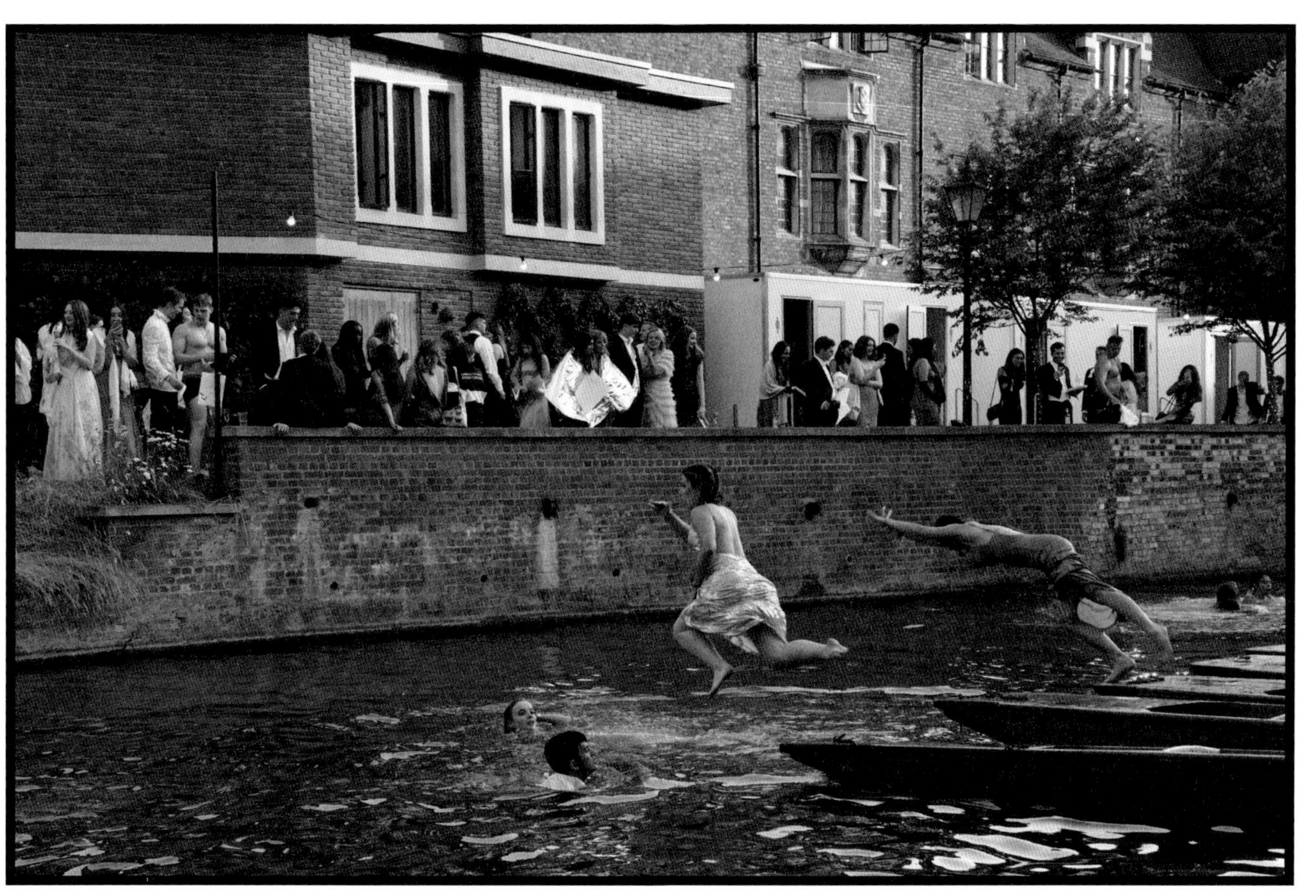

Magdalene May Ball, 21 June 2023

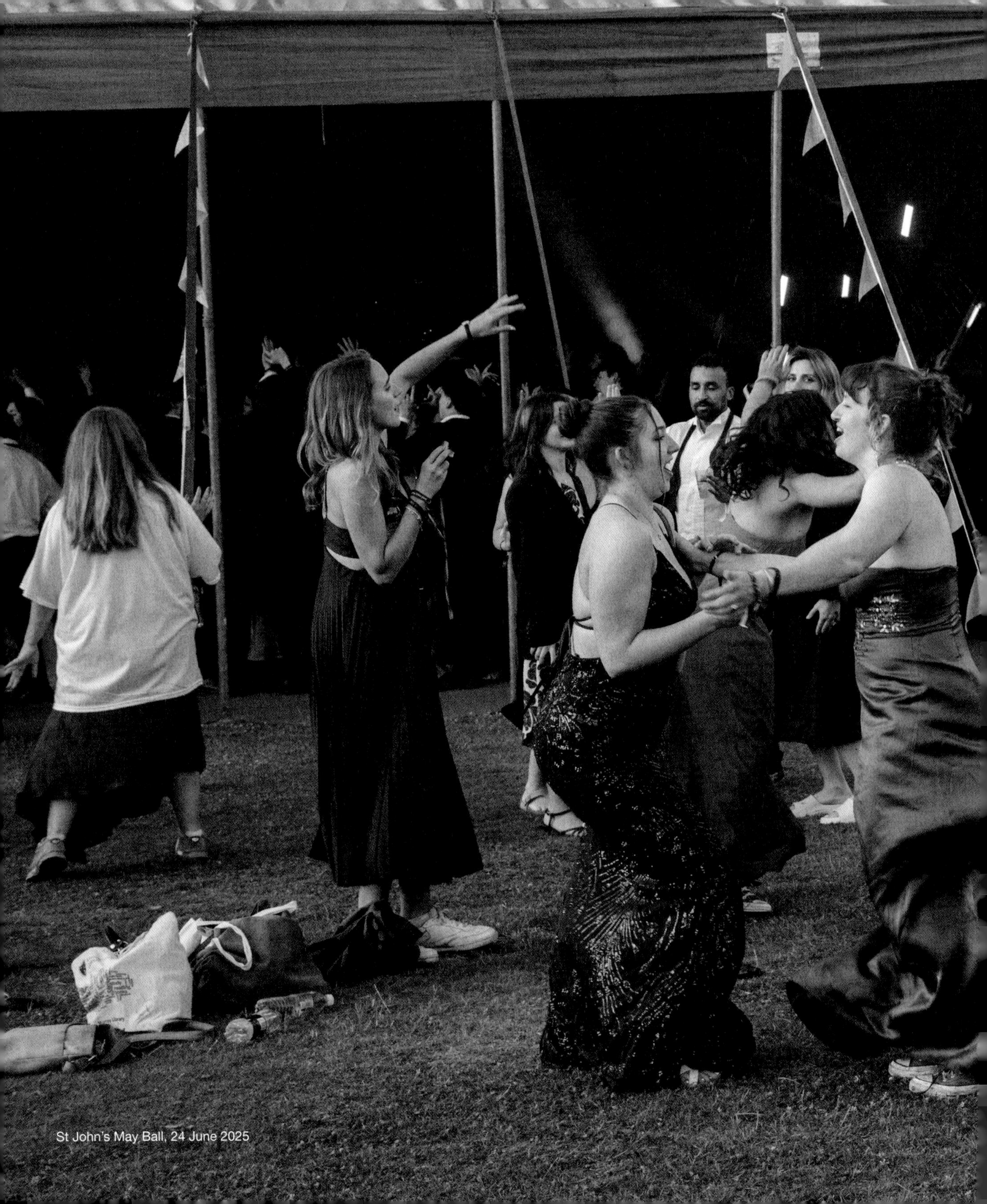

St John's May Ball, 24 June 2025

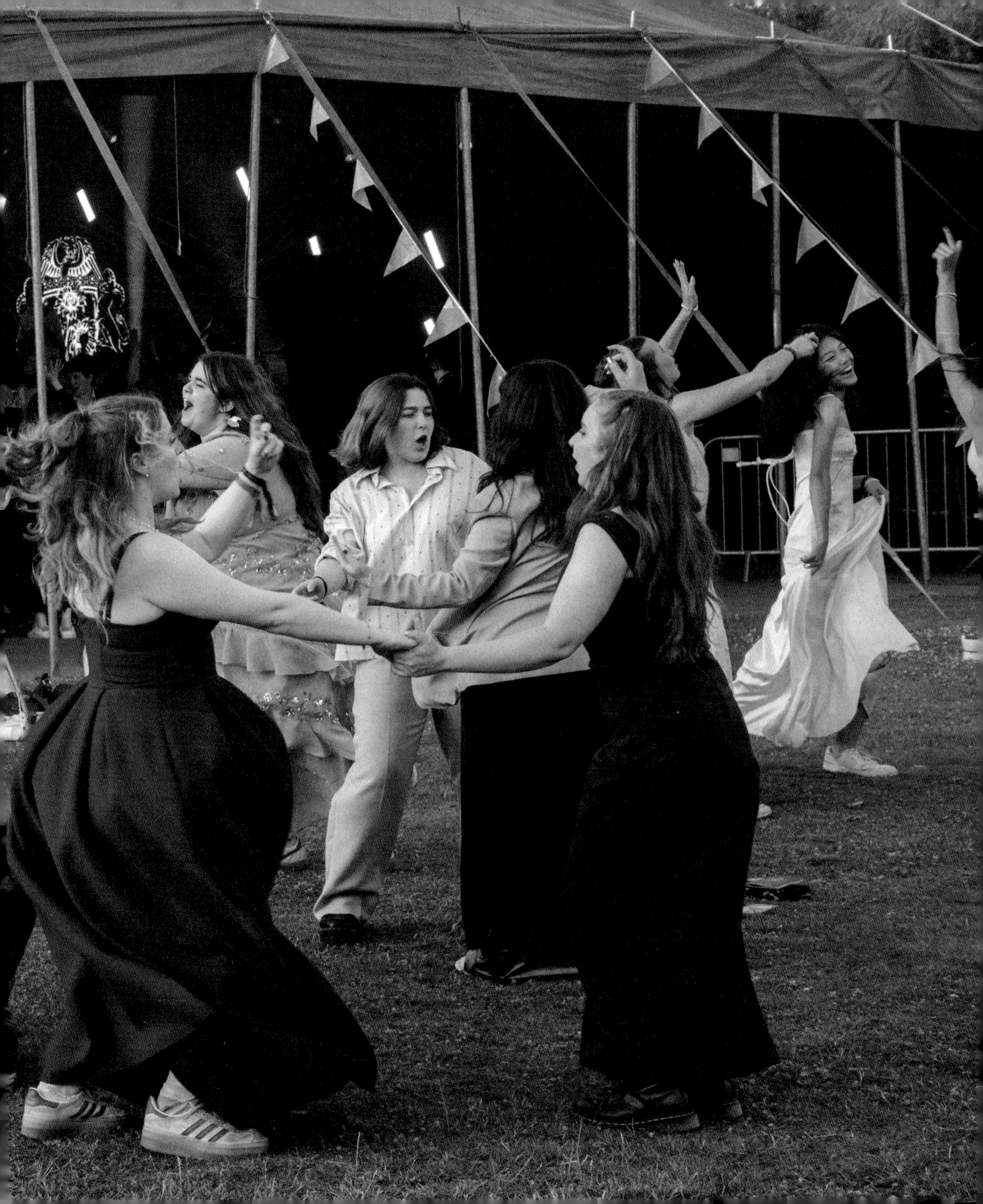

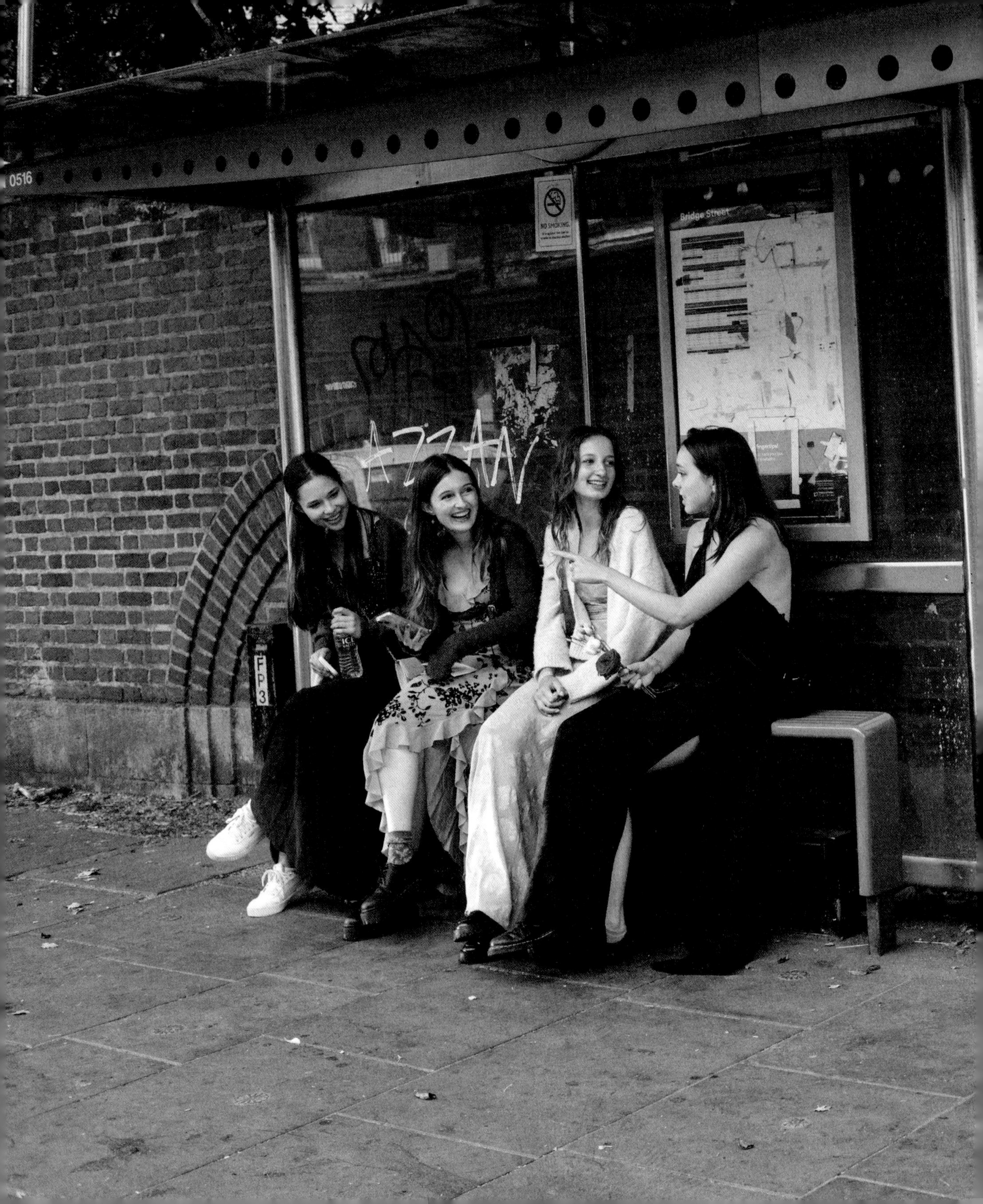
0516
NO SMOKING.
Bridge Street
FP3

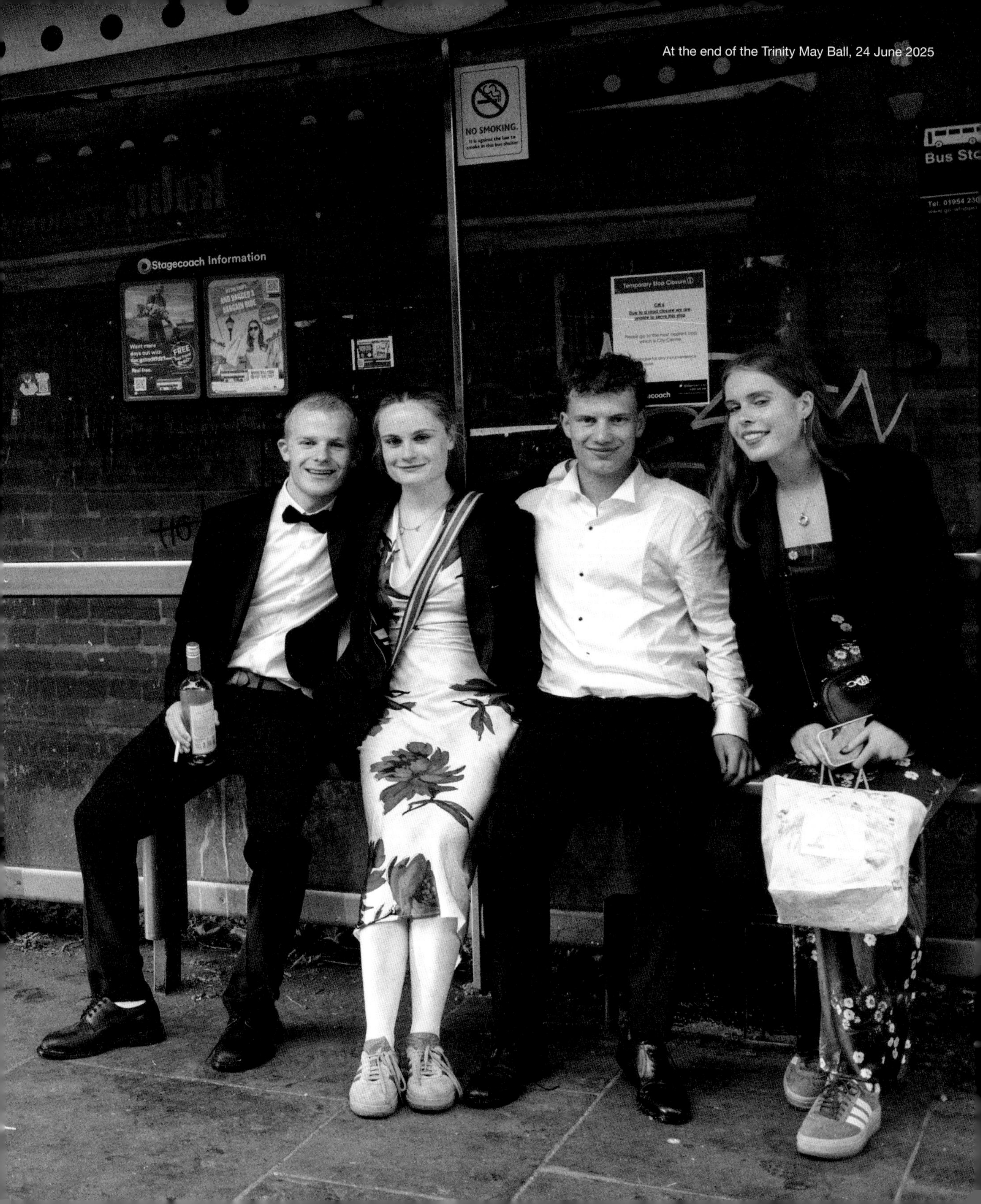

At the end of the Trinity May Ball, 24 June 2025

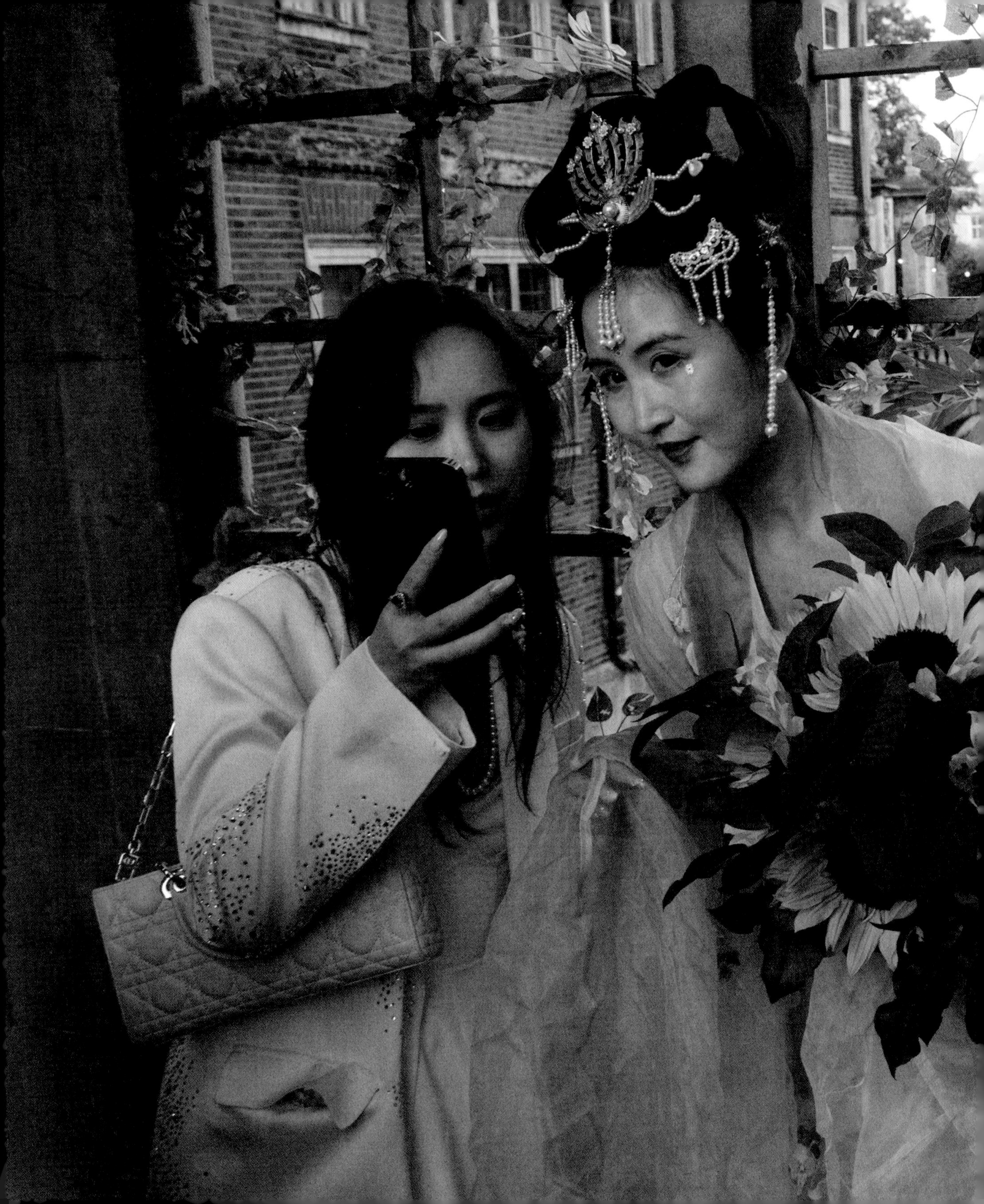

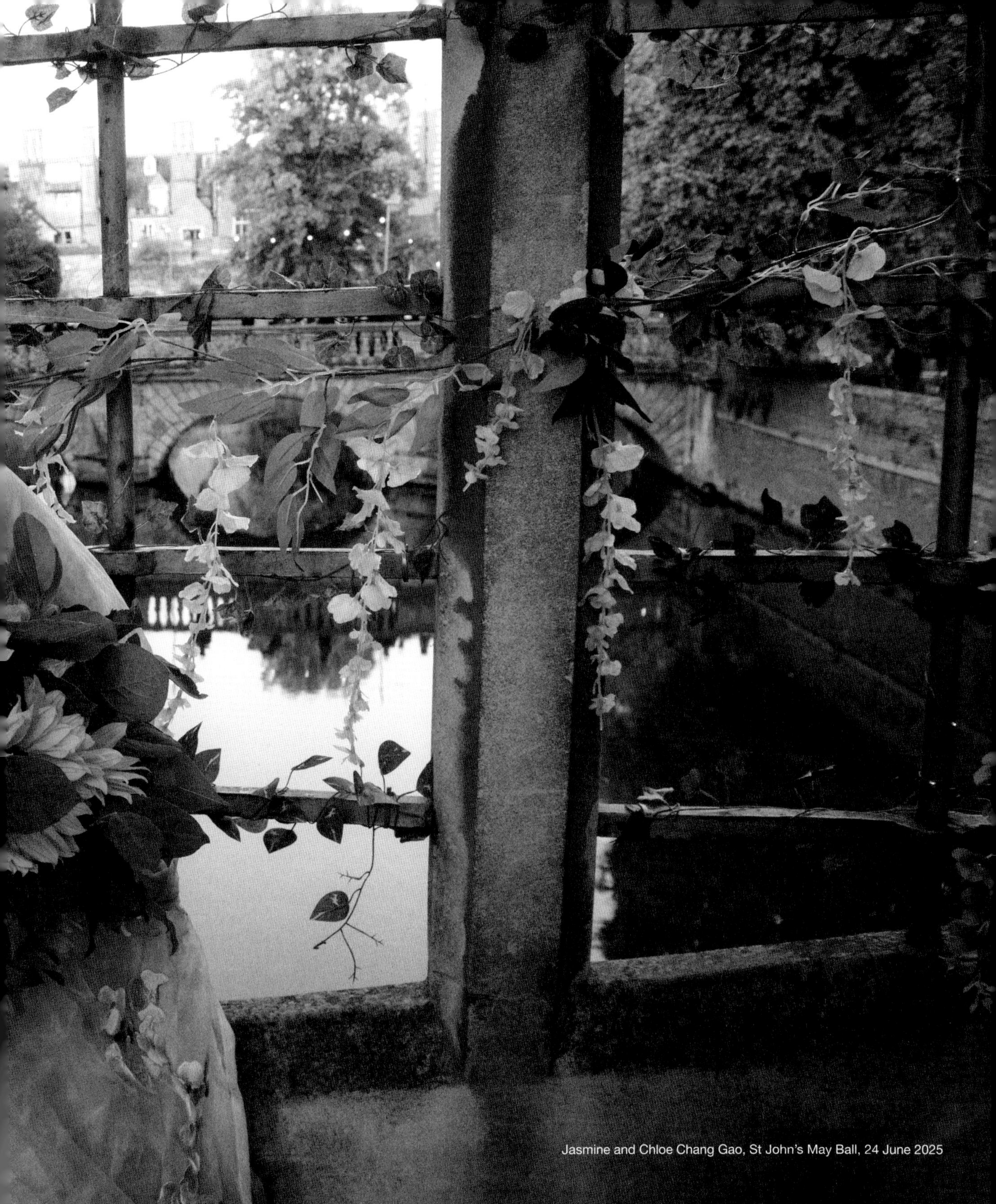

Jasmine and Chloe Chang Gao, St John's May Ball, 24 June 2025

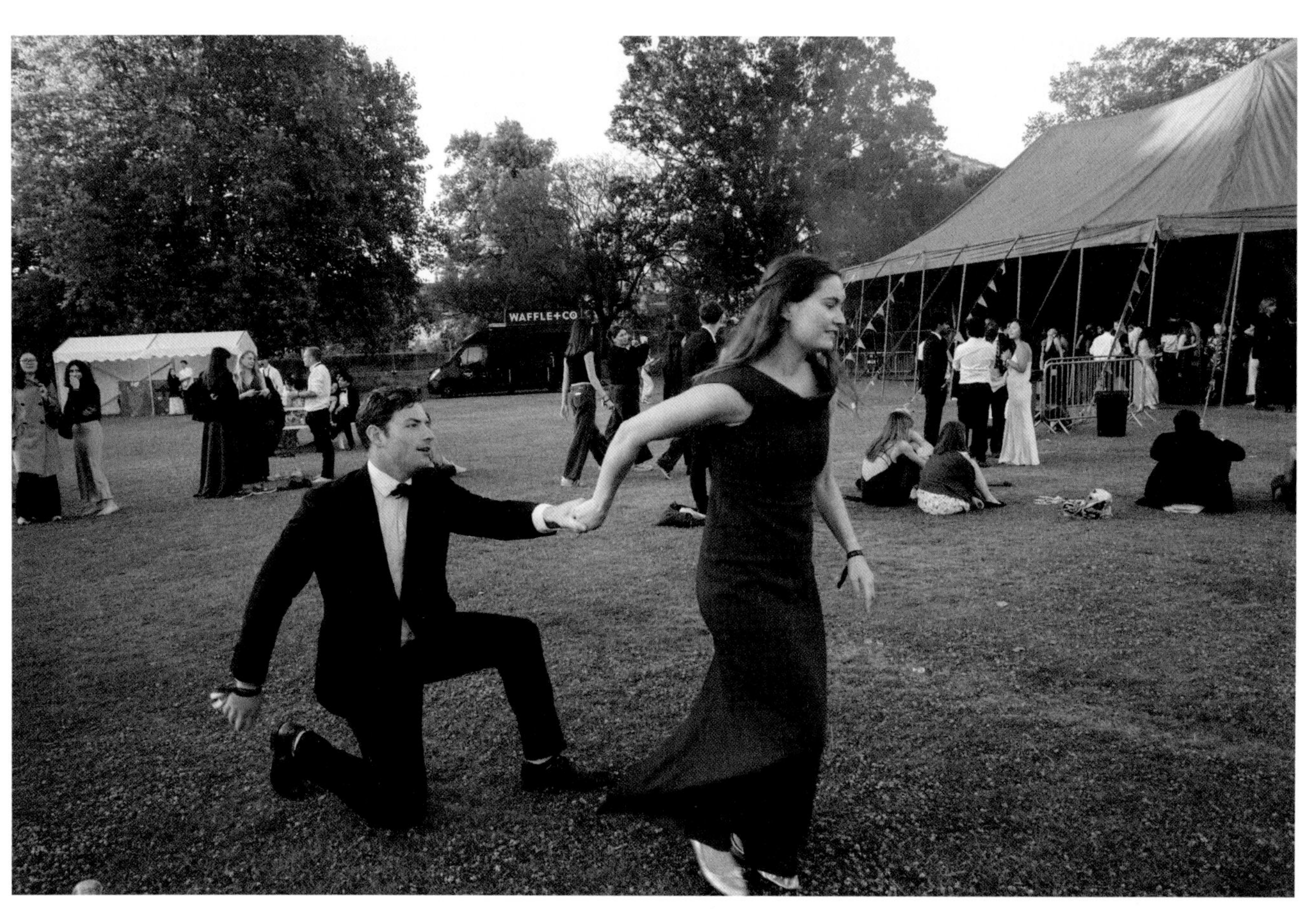

St John's May Ball, 24 June 2025

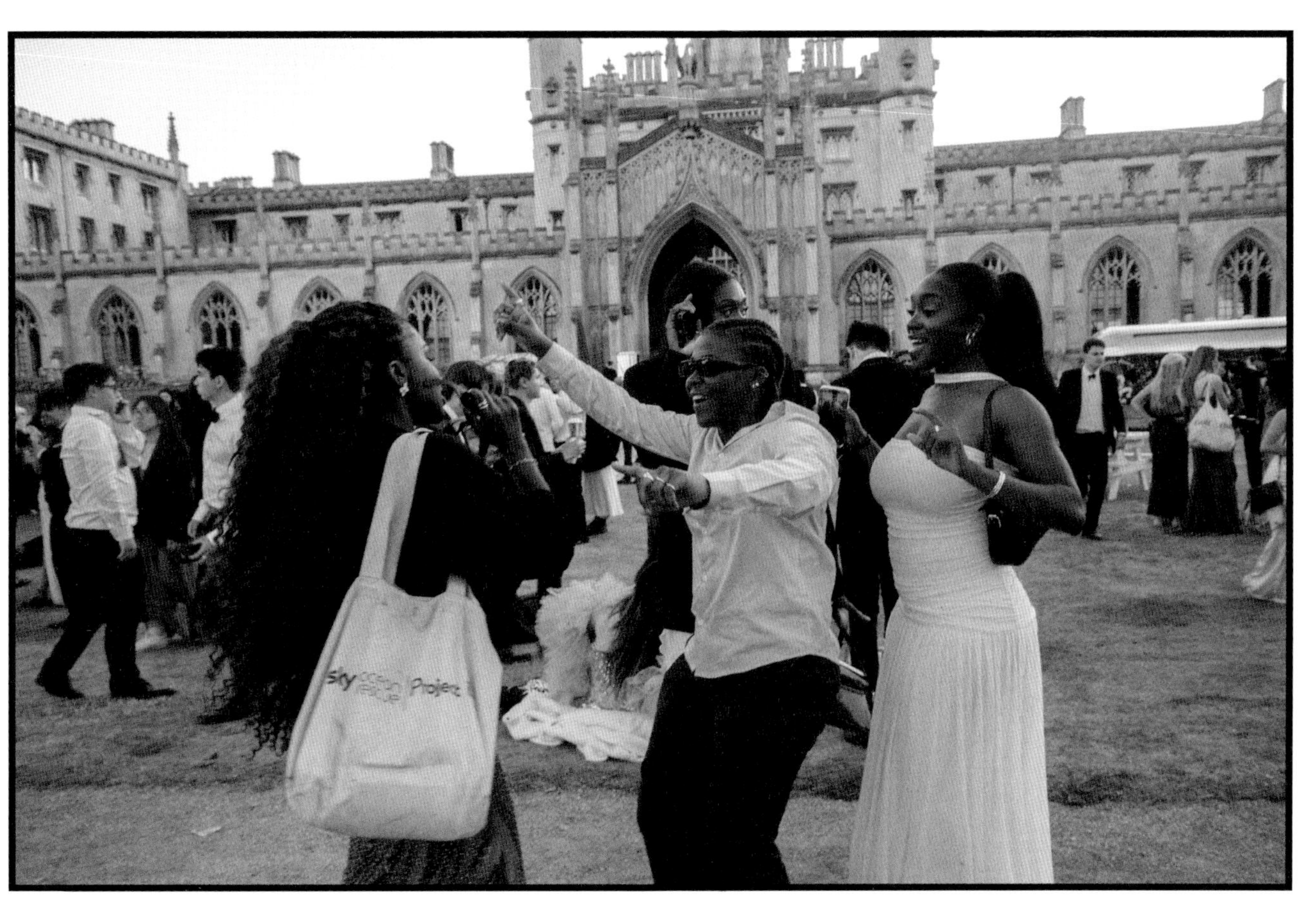

St John's May Ball, 24 June 2025

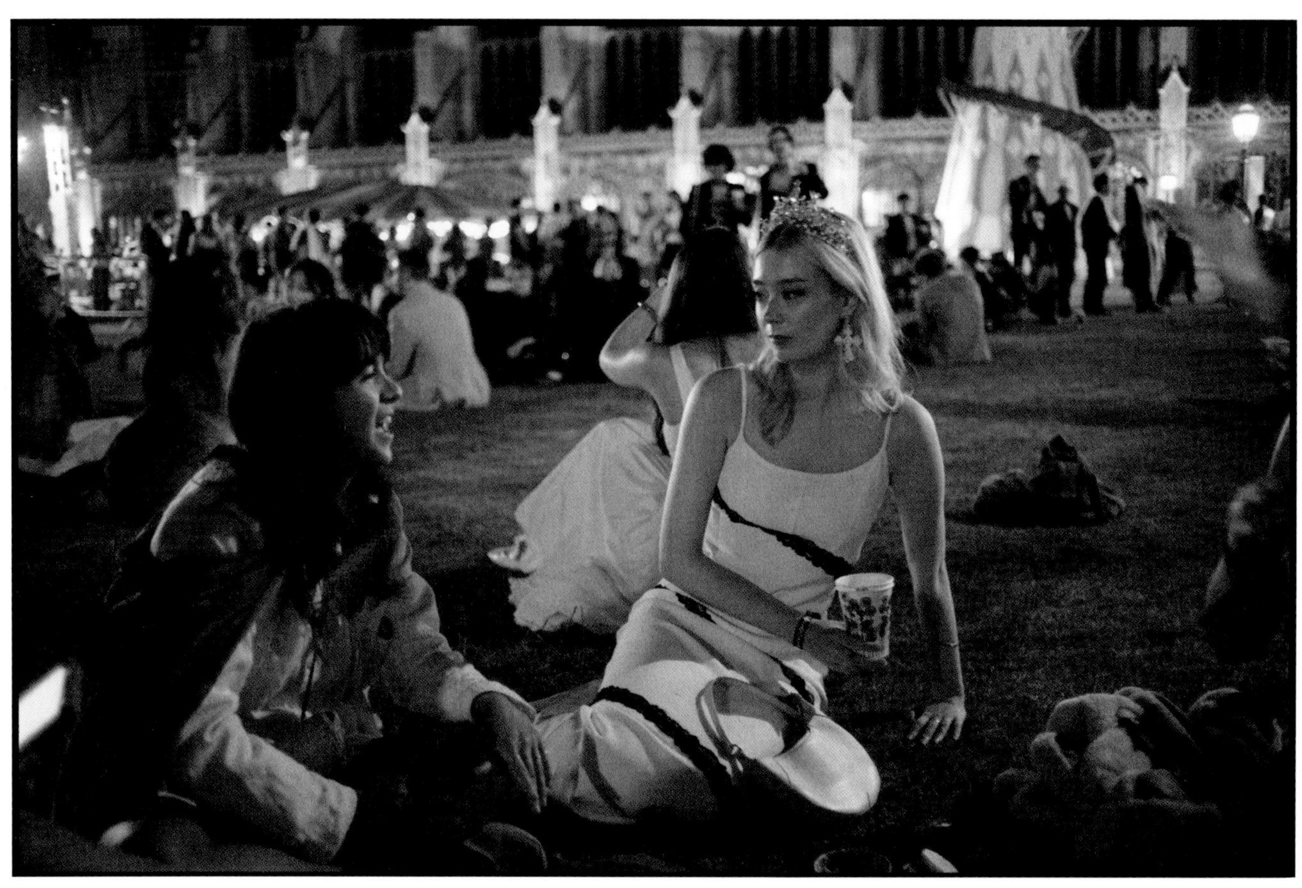

Federica Panpana and Tilly Middlehurst, The King's Affair, King's College, 25 June 2025

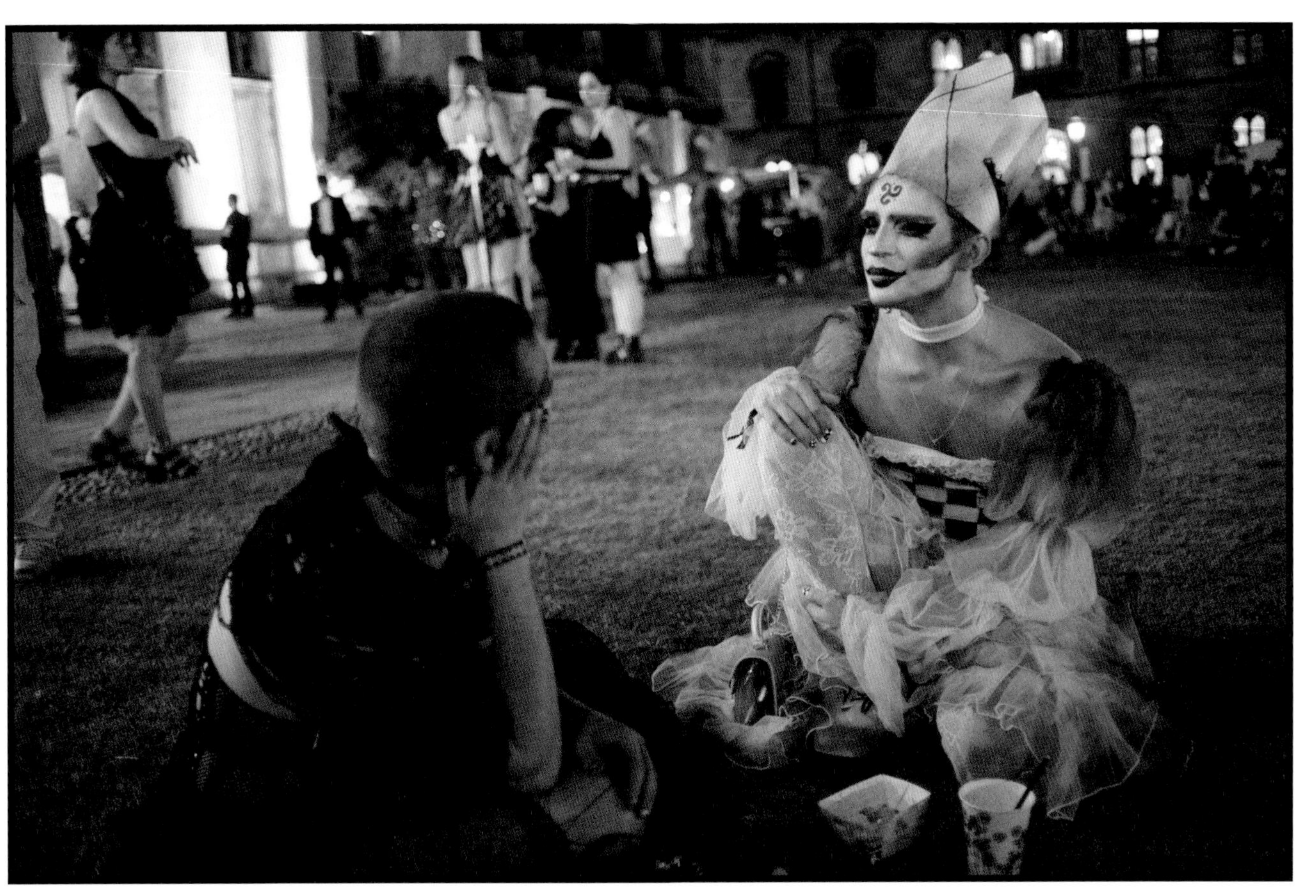

The King's Affair, King's College, 25 June 2025

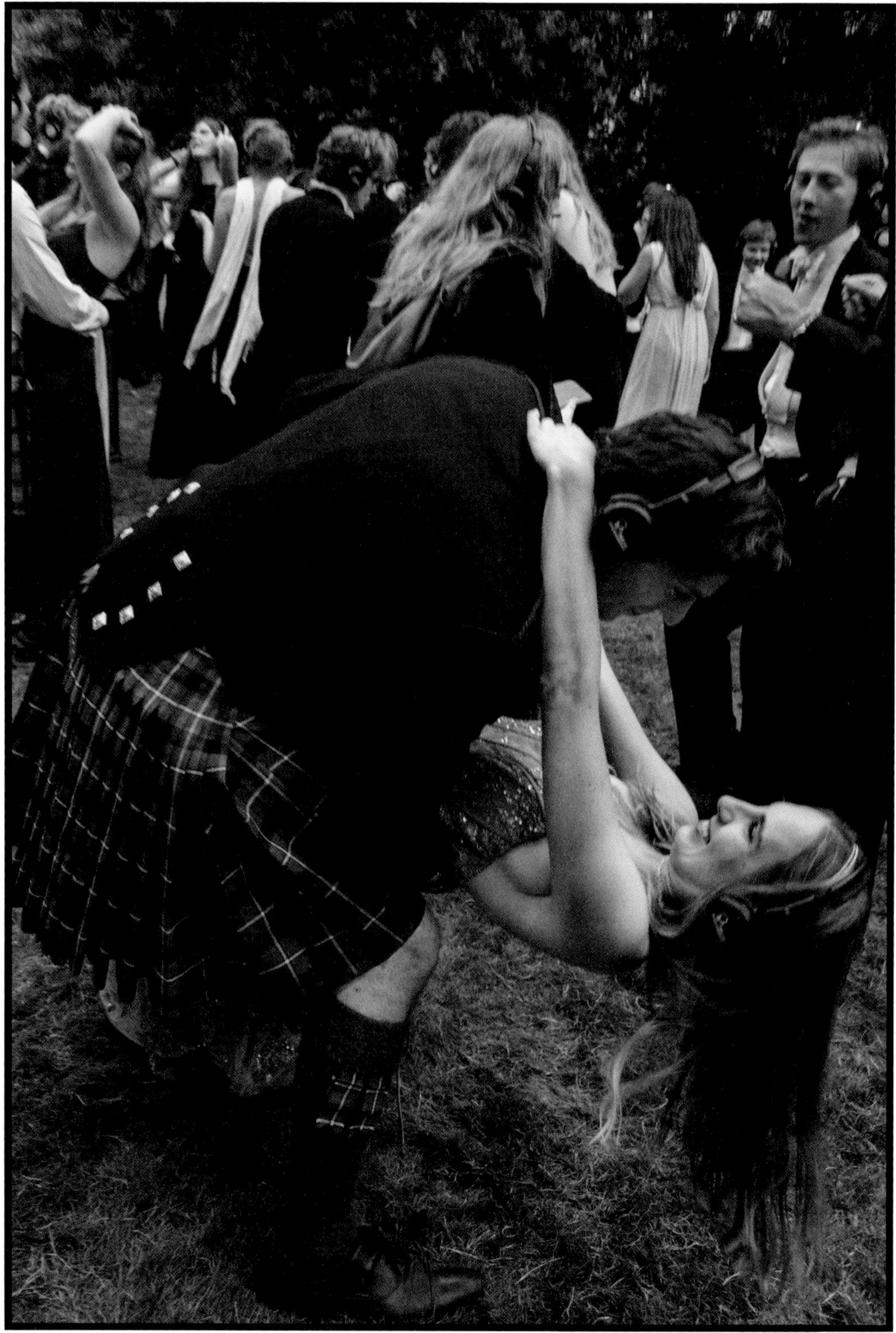

Magdalene May Ball, 25 June 2025

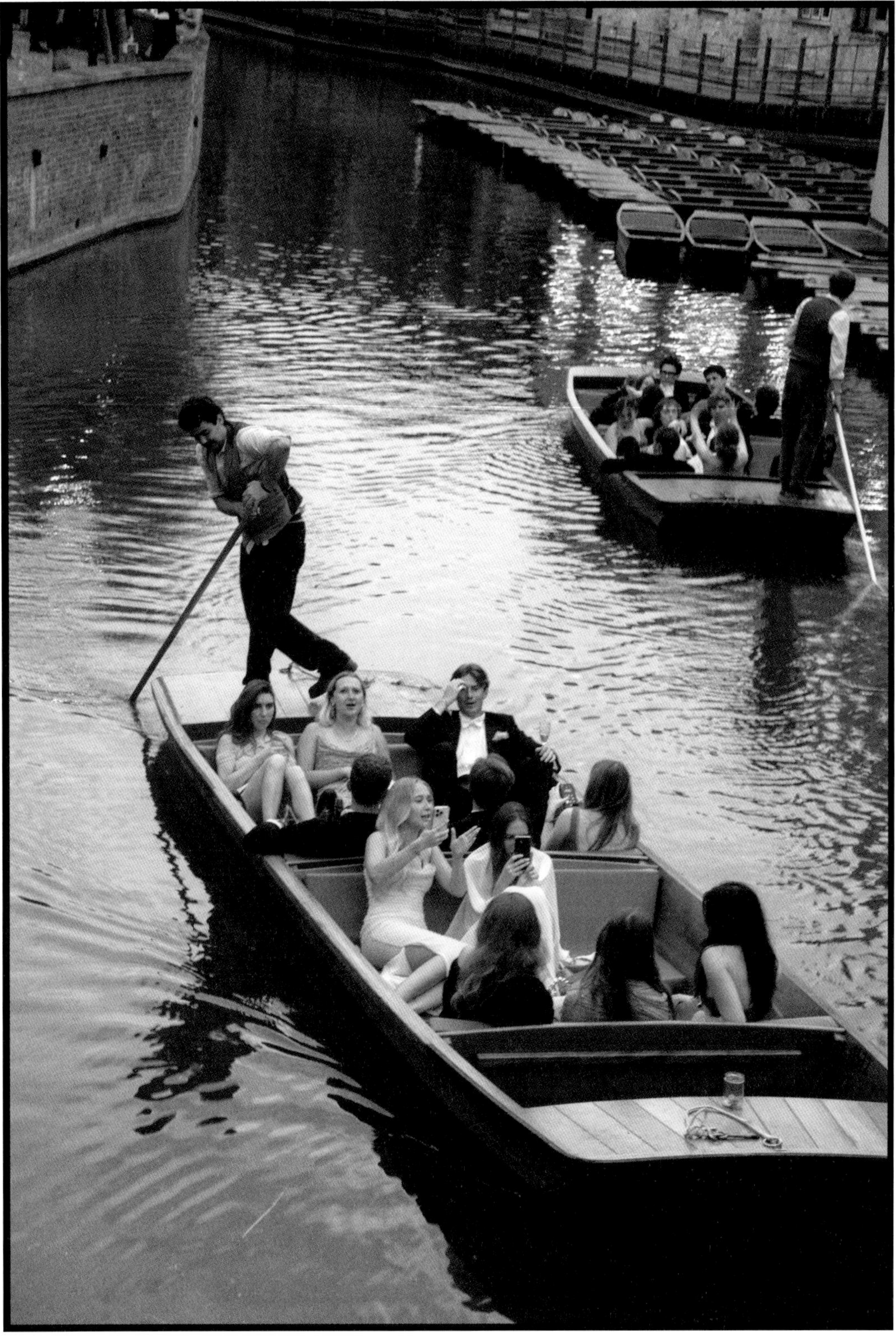

Magdalene May Ball, 25 June 2025

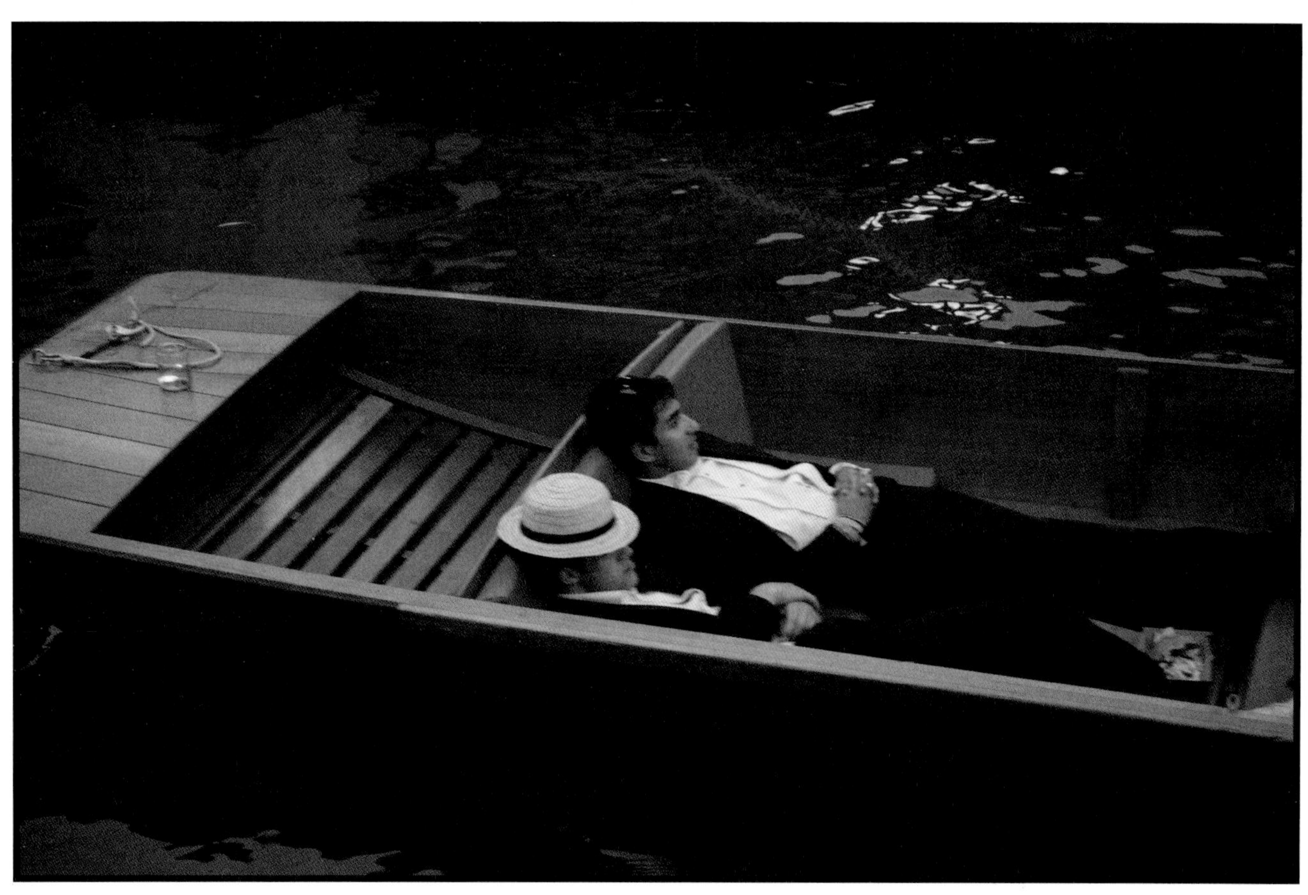

Magdalene May Ball, 25 June 2025

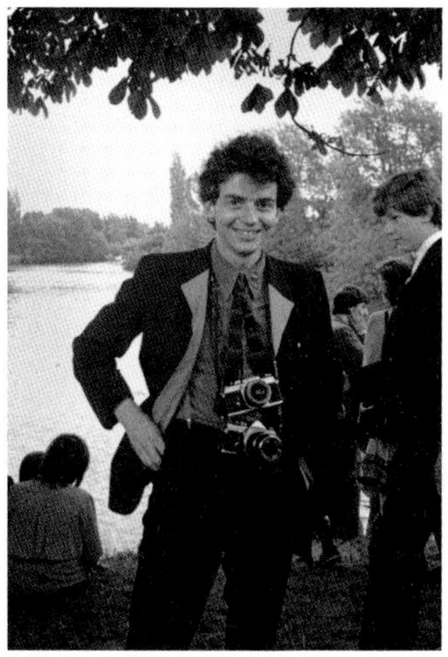

Dafydd Jones, June 1981
Photograph by Nicholas Coleridge

Front cover image: Trinity Hall Ball, 1983
Back cover image: Climbing into Trinity May Ball, 15 June 1981

ISBN: 978 1 78884 356 0

A CIP catalogue record for this book is available from the British Library

The author and publisher gratefully acknowledge the permission granted to reproduce the copyright material in this book. Every effort has been made to trace copyright holders and to obtain their permission for the use of copyright material. The publisher apologises for any errors or omissions in the text and would be grateful if notified of any corrections that should be incorporated in future reprints or editions of this book.

Editor: Sue Bennett
Designers: Steve Farrow, Mariona Vilarós
Production Manager: Simon Walsh
Reprographics Manager: Corban Wilkin

EU GPSR Authorised Representative:
Easy Access System Europe Oü, 16879218
Address: Mustamäe tee 50, 10621 Tallinn, Estonia
Email: gpsr@easproject.com Tel: +358 40 500 3575

Printed in Slovenia by Green Leaf Production
for ACC Art Books Ltd, Woodbridge, Suffolk, UK

www.accartbooks.com

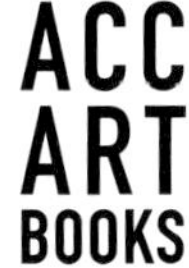

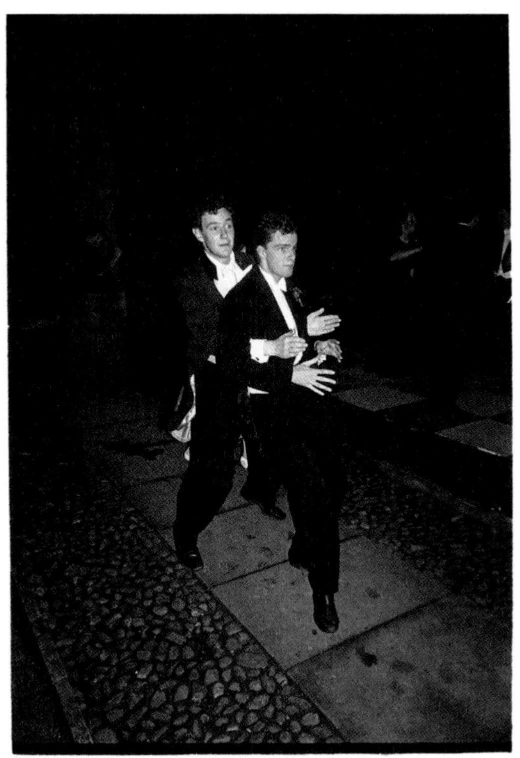

Dominic Armstrong and Charles Prideaux, Magdalene May Ball, 17 June 1987